Is Freedom Worth Dying For?

A Theological Tribute to Charlie Kirk

by
Tim Cantrell

© 2025 Tim Cantrell

Johannesburg, South Africa

ISBN
Paper: 978-1-0492-1817-5
Epub: 978-1-0492-2025-3

Scripture quotes are from the 1995 New American Standard Bible © Lockman Foundation. Used by permission.

No part of this publication may be reproduced, or stored in a retrieval system or transmitted, in any form or by any means, without the prior permission of the author and publisher Tim Cantrell.

(Original cover artwork by our friends at https://mediaonx.com/)

"And they overcame him by the blood of the Lamb and by the word of their testimony, and they did not love their lives to the death." (Revelation 12:11)

> The Son of God goes forth to war,
> A kingly crown to gain;
> His blood-red banner streams afar:
> Who follows in His train?
> Who best can drink his cup of woe,
> Triumphant over pain,
> Who patient bears his cross below,
> He follows in His train.
>
> The martyr first, whose eagle eye
> Could pierce beyond the grave,
> Who saw his Master in the sky,
> And called to Him to save:
> Like Him, with pardon on his tongue,
> In midst of mortal pain,
> He prayed for them that did the wrong:
> Who follows in his train?
>
> A glorious band, the chosen few
> On whom the Spirit came,
> Twelve valiant saints, their hope they knew,
> And mocked the cross and flame.
> They met the tyrant's brandished steel,
> The lion's gory mane,
> They bowed their necks, the death to feel:
> Who follows in their train?
>
> A noble army, men and boys,
> The matron and the maid,
> Around the Savior's throne rejoice,
> In robes of light arrayed.
> They climbed the steep ascent of heaven,
> Through peril, toil, and pain:
> O God, to us may grace be given
> To follow in their train.

(Reginald Heber, 1812)

TABLE OF CONTENTS

Introduction 7

Chapter 1 – Freedom is from God 15

Chapter 2 – Freedom is Defined by God's Word 29

Chapter 3 – Freedom is a Treasure 35

Chapter 4 – Freedom is Fragile 45

Chapter 5 – Freedom Requires Co-Belligerency 59

Appendix A – Kirk's Global Impact 69

Appendix B – A Prayer for America from Africa 77

Appendix C – Grudem's Case for Public Theology 81

Postscript on Kirk-Elliot Parallels 92

Gospel Message 93

Introduction

It was Wednesday evening, 10 September, here in Johannesburg. We had just ended our church small group by closing in prayer. Suddenly, someone remarked that Charlie Kirk had just been shot. We turned on the news and watched in stunned silence, as this peaceful, unarmed, bold and clear ambassador for Christ was assassinated in front of thousands of students just for speaking the truth.

The plain white T-shirt he wore, about to be stained by his own innocent blood, read, "Freedom". Charlie was shot at the very moment when he made his trademark gesture of putting down the microphone to listen carefully to his questioner. Yet his answer to that final question never came.

Instead of silencing Charlie's voice, that bullet amplified his testimony a thousandfold. As his brave wife, Erika, would declare to his enemies two days later, "You have no idea what you have just unleashed." Charlie came in the name of the Unconquerable Christ, "The stone the builders rejected has become the chief cornerstone" (Acts 4:11). There is a light that shines from that empty tomb, and the darkness cannot overcome it (Jn. 1:5).

We serve a risen Lord who defeated death, who said that even the "gates of Hades" could not stop Him from building His Church (Matt. 16:18). "But God!" are the two best words in the Bible – bursting with hope, because our God is so sovereign that He overturns the worst tragedies, brings life through death, triumph through defeat, resurrection through crucifixion.

Jesus said, "Unless a grain of wheat falls into the ground and dies, it remains alone; but if it dies, it produces much grain" (Jn. 12:24). Tertullian, renowned apologist of the early church, said, "The blood of the martyrs is the seed of the Church." Or as Kierkegaard wrote, "The tyrant dies and his rule is over, the martyr dies and his rule begins."

Jim Elliot famously said, "He is no fool who gives what he cannot keep to gain what he cannot lose." Just as God used Elliot's death in the 20th century to raise up a whole new generation of missionaries, we pray that God will use Charlie Kirk's death to inspire a new wave of warriors for Christ.

For Faith or Freedom?

Did Charlie die for Christ or for freedom? Did he die for his faith or his political views? Yes, both, *and in that order*. Every freedom fighter isn't necessarily a Christian; but Charlie was. His faith drove him into politics. He was a patriot who gave his life defending our liberties out of love for his Lord and love for his neighbour, which Jesus taught were the two greatest commandments, the very sum of all God's Law (Matt. 22:37-39).

A faith that stays cloistered in private and never goes public is weak or false. There is nothing to admire about a faith divorced from ethics, morality, economics and politics. Moments before Charlie was murdered for answering a question about transgenders, he was boldly preaching the gospel: "It's not just intra-biblical evidence, but extra-biblical evidence that Jesus Christ was a real person. He lived a perfect life, he was crucified, died and rose on the third day, and he is Lord and God over all."

Public Theology

After two centuries of pietistic isolation, it is time for the Church to come out of our ghetto and follow Charlie's example, recovering a biblically robust Public Theology (see Appendix C for more on this). After seeing Charlie in action on college campuses, these Scriptures keep jumping out at me:

> *Does not wisdom call, and understanding lift up her voice? On top of the heights beside the way, where the paths meet, she takes her stand; beside the gates, at the opening to the city, at the*

> *entrance of the doors, she cries out: 'To you, O men, I call…'*
> *…Wisdom calls from the tops of the heights of the city, 'Whoever is naïve, let him turn in here!'* (Prov. 8:1-4; 9:3-4).
>
> *Your commandment makes me wiser than my enemies, for it is ever with me. I have more understanding than all my teachers, for Your testimonies are my meditation. I understand more than the aged, for I keep Your precepts* (Ps. 119:98-100).
>
> *Now therefore, O kings, be wise; be warned, O rulers of the earth* (Ps. 2:10).

The Bible is not shy about going public in the marketplace of ideas. Charlie exemplified that, as he studied the questions of our secular age, he understood the competing worldviews and graciously refuted each lie with biblical truth. Consider: Mr. Kirk was killed for confronting the very same gender ideology which leading pastors of our day have gone soft on, even advising that we attend gay weddings and take a gift![1]

Society loves a private, compartmentalised Church that will leave them alone, unbothered and unrebuked, with no prophetic voice heralding the Word of God. Satan loves it when believers are retreating instead of advancing for Christ in this world, not "turning upside down" their city like the apostles of old (Acts 17:6-7). The demons are delighted when we stop preaching God's Law and calling lost sinners to repent of the specific sins of our culture so that they might come to Christ and be saved.

Lawless Pulpits

In the aftermath of Kirk's murder, Pastor David Mitzenmacher warns:[2]

---

[1] https://www.christianitytoday.com/2024/01/alistair-begg-lgbtq-gay-wedding-advice-radio-sermon-truth/.
[2] https://founders.org/articles/courage-and-clarity-in-the-pulpit/.

In one of the most morally charged moments in recent memory, too many pulpits flinched. Their silence and equivocation reveal a deeper sickness in evangelicalism: the neglect of God's moral law. A pulpit without the law cannot name evil as evil and goodness as good. It cannot convict the conscience or point sinners to the only Savior. And a lawless pulpit cannot stand against a lawless age.

...When preachers refuse to exercise the second use of the law, it leaves the people of God morally disarmed. It leaves our society without the categories necessary to make sense of the moral chaos that increasingly defines our age. If the pulpit will not name lawlessness—specifically and boldly—then who will?

This past weekend was an inflection point. The eyes of the nation were, in many cases, fixed upon the pulpit. Praise the Lord that many churches were faithful to the whole counsel of God's Word. But far too many pulpits faltered. Instead of the bold proclamation of God's law and gospel, many congregations received evasion wrapped in the veneer of pietism.

The choice before the church is stark: either we will retreat into silence as the next generation is catechized by lies, or we will love our neighbors by working to restrain that which God calls evil and promote that which God calls good. One path leads to irrelevance and judgment. The other leads to faithfulness, and by God's mercy, revival.

Capitulation vs. Courage

Brad Klassen, an elder at Grace Community Church and professor at The Master's Seminary, wrote this after Charlie's death:

Where we are today as a culture is not by accident. Sadly, vast portions of professing Christianity in the West began to capitulate to cultural degradation decades ago. Compromisers

> *believed that the best way to "win" sinners over was to eliminate from their message anything offensive. Certainly, Roman Catholic and mainline Protestantism led the way.*
>
> *But significant evangelical ministries like Fuller Theological Seminary and Christianity Today also went silent and refused to confront the culture. Then they began to suggest openly that these movements could be syncretized with Christianity. Then they began to attack directly those like John MacArthur and Charlie Kirk who spoke out against these ideologies. Learn from all of this: we must not bow.*[3]

A longtime missionary friend of mine, serving in a closed country, wrote this:

> <u>Charlie Kirk, First American Christian Martyr</u>: Wednesday, 10 September, will go down as a pivotal day (a turning point?) in church history with the assassination of Charlie Kirk. His death in the public square, standing for Jesus, marks the first (at least well-known) Christian martyr on American soil. You can put him in a modern <u>Foxe's Book of Martyrs</u>.

Charlie's Pastor

Rob McCoy of Calvary Chapel became Charlie's pastor, mentor and dear friend. McCoy sums up Charlie's legacy and the need for books like mine:

> We must be vigilant to protect our freedom. But the pulpits of America have lulled the sheep to sleep by truncating the gospel and embracing Gnosticism. Charlie Kirk was the most misunderstood missionary in America because he saw politics as an on-ramp to Jesus.

---

[3] From a 14 Sept. e-mail sent to his flock group.

Charlie contended for this young generation that had been saddled with the debt of the largess living of the previous generations. ...These kids are the most indebted, drug-addicted and depressed generation in America. And we've abandoned them because we 'don't do politics'. Good government happens with good people; but the churches haven't discipled people to engage in a representative form of government to protect that freedom.

These kids in America, who were trapped in a pagan system of secular education, being indoctrinated by this stupidity, were set free from captivity and slavery by this modern-day Moses (Charlie Kirk). ...Charlie told them, 'You're in the freest nation on the face of the earth; but liberty is one generation away from being obliterated.' And they listened! ...Now they're all chanting, "I am Charlie Kirk!"[4]

Time will tell how lasting Charlie's impact will be; but we pray it would take deep root. The aim of this book is to help fill that void in discipling the next generation of responsible Christian citizens.

Persecution Guaranteed

Time and again Christ and His apostles prepared us for this hour, for facing a Satanically inspired, hate-filled world in these last days before His return. My nephew attends a California state university, where he said that the student reaction to Charlie Kirk's murder was dancing and celebration?!

Behold, I am sending you out as sheep in the midst of wolves.... You will be hated by all for My name's sake. ... Do not think that I have come to bring peace to the earth. I have not come to bring peace, but a sword. ... If the world hates you, know that it has

---

[4]https://www.youtube.com/watch?v=I1PdXmbgxCA.

hated Me before it hated you. ...A servant is not greater than his master.'

Indeed, all who desire to live a godly life in Christ Jesus will be persecuted.... Beloved, do not be surprised at the fiery trial when it comes upon you to test you, as though something strange were happening to you.

...Now I rejoice in my sufferings for your sake, and in my flesh I am filling up what is lacking in Christ's afflictions for the sake of His body, that is, the Church. ...For it has been granted to you that for the sake of Christ you should not only believe in Him but also suffer for His sake.

...Some were tortured, refusing to accept release, so that they might rise again to a better life. Others suffered mocking and flogging, and even chains and imprisonment. They were stoned, they were sawn in two, they were killed with the sword. They went about in skins of sheep and goats, destitute, afflicted, mistreated—of whom the world was not worthy.[5]

My Aim

Charlie knew, much better than most, that we're living through a time of massive cultural upheaval and an onslaught of godless worldviews and deadly ideologies. If we do not recognise and refute these lies, "destroying" and "taking them captive to the obedience of Christ", they will keep shaping our instincts and our imaginations (2 Cor. 10:5).

We must "understand the times", renew our minds lest we conform, and plant our roots deep in a biblical worldview (1 Chron. 12:32; Eph. 4:14-16; Rom. 12:2). Ideas have consequences, so we must win the battle at the level of beliefs, not just behaviour (Col. 2:8).

---

[5] Matt. 10:16-39; Jn. 15:18-25; 2 Tim. 3:12; 1 Pet. 4:12; Col. 1:24; Php. 1:29; Heb. 11:35-38.

Some of us have a pastoral calling, others a political calling, while most are called to more ordinary vocations (at home, school, work, business, etc.). Every church and believer will have different applications in how they stand up for human freedom; but if these principles are biblical, we cannot ignore them. We don't have to agree with Charlie Kirk or his organisation on every doctrine to still "hold men like him in high regard" because he gave his life for Christ and His cause (Php. 2:30).

As a fellow American, I also write with a heavy burden for my homeland, though I have now lived over half of my life serving Christ in South Africa. Yet the longer I live overseas, the more I appreciate American exceptionalism and that nation's unparalleled role in global missions and freedom (see Appendix B).

Read on to learn *five battle cries for Christians to be champions of liberty* in every sphere of life, following in Charlie Kirk's courageous footsteps as he followed Christ (1 Cor. 11:1; Heb. 13:7).

For a man of Mr. Kirk's stature, the forthcoming biographies, documentaries and movies from insiders will tell his story far better than an outsider like me, as many eloquent testimonies and his unprecedented memorial service have already done.

Nonetheless, I offer this humble tribute from across the Atlantic to encourage Charlie's family and followers, and to thank the Author of liberty for all He is teaching me, my family and my church from this modern-day Christian hero.

Tim Cantrell
October 2025
Johannesburg

(1) Freedom is from God

Made in His Image

Historian Dean Curry notes, "The roots of tyranny are found in man's denial of God's transcendence."[6] If freedom is not from God, it must come from dictators, the state, or whomever claims to be all-powerful. Yet Scripture says otherwise. Listen to Genesis 1:26-28:

Then God said, "Let us make man in our image, after our likeness. And let them have dominion over the fish of the sea and over the birds of the heavens and over the livestock and over all the earth and over every creeping thing that creeps on the earth."

So God created man in his own image, in the image of God he created him; male and female he created them. And God blessed them. And God said to them, "Be fruitful and multiply and fill the earth and subdue it, and have dominion over the fish of the sea and over the birds of the heavens and over every living thing that moves on the earth."

To be human is to reflect God. That is why we speak of God's communicable attributes, those traits of His that are share-able, translatable to us. For example, "Be holy as I am holy" (Lev. 19). God is loving, He is good, He is just, He is wise, and so must we be. And God is also free, as are we, made in His likeness.

God's Freedom

Theologians for centuries have taught that freedom is one of God's attributes, that God does whatever He pleases according to His holy will. God is unconstrained and unrestrained by anything outside Himself. He is the most liberated and only being in the universe who

---

[6] p. 143, *A World Without Tyranny*.

is totally free: Psalm 115:3 (unlike the dead, enslaved idols), "Our God is in the heavens; He does whatever He pleases."

Psalm 135:6, "Whatever the LORD pleases, He does, in heaven and in earth, in the seas and in all deeps." Daniel 4, "He does according to His will in the host of heaven, and among the inhabitants of earth; and no one can ward off His hand or say to Him, 'What have you done?'" (cf. Job. 42:2; Isa.. 43:13; 45:9; Ps. 33:11; Prov. 21:1; Rom. 9)

God's freedom is infinite and inherent as an independent Creator. Our freedom, as dependent creatures, is finite, derived, relative, and limited. Since the Fall, our freedom is depraved, corrupted, and badly damaged. But it is not erased. Fallen man is still made in God's image (Gen. 9:6).

And we are still called to "rule, subdue," and cultivate the earth, as His vice-regents, with a subordinate authority under Him. That means God has entrusted humans with moral agency, the power and duty to bring about results on this earth and in our vocations to which He calls us.

Inalienable Rights

Recently, a U.S. senator, Tim Kaine (Democrat from Virginia) had the ignorance and audacity to say, "The notion that rights don't come from laws and don't come from the government but come from the Creator — that's what the Iranian government believes."[7] This elected official could not have picked words more diametrically opposed to our nation's own founding document.[8]

---

[7] https://www.lifenews.com/2025/09/05/tim-kaine-claims-rights-come-from-government-not-god/?utm_source=chatgpt.com.
[8] As the Declaration of Independence begins: "We hold these truths to be self-evident, that all men are created equal, that they are endowed by their Creator with certain unalienable Rights, that among these are Life, Liberty and the pursuit of Happiness. That to secure these rights, Governments are instituted among Men...." (July 4th, 1776). Is this more John Locke than Bible? Historian Glenn Sunshine shows where we can and cannot agree biblically with Locke, plus the extent of his influence upon America's founding fathers:

Let's be very clear: No human government or laws bestow on people their rights or liberties. If rulers want to be blessed, they should recognise what God has already given mankind – inherent, fixed rights as His sacred, unique image-bearers. If civil authorities want to be cursed, they will deny man those created, inalienable rights.

Psalm 8 declares the royal, God-given dignity of humanity: "What is man that You are mindful of him? Yet you have made him a little lower than the angels, and crowned him with glory and honour, and made him ruler over creation...." There is no more dignified creature in the universe.

Not even the most beautiful plants or most adorable pets, not the most brilliant horse, dolphin or monkey – none of them can escape their plant/animal nature and instincts, to which they are held captive. They have no soul or conscience, which only mankind has been given as image-bearers of the Almighty. To bear God's likeness means volition and will, a freedom to choose.

Curry again points out that it is no accident that the first freedom in America's Bill of Rights is the freedom of religion:

> *The Framers of American democracy realized that freedom of religion was basic to all other freedoms and therefore was the bedrock of democracy.*
>
> *...The right to freedom of conscience is premised not upon science, nor upon utility, nor upon pride of species. Rather, it is premised upon the inviolable (God-given) dignity of the human person. It is the foundation of, and is integrally related to, all other rights and freedoms.*
>
> *...The inviolability of the conscience is <u>the</u> foundational right from which all others flow. ...Religious belief is an ever-present*

---

https://www.amazon.com/Slaying-Leviathan-Government-Resistance-Christian/dp/195241072X/.

threat to the tyrant. ...continually reminding mankind that human power is less than ultimate.[9]

Biblical Cultures

Vishal Mangalwadi is perhaps India's foremost Christian intellectual. He wrote *The Book That Made Your World*, in which he describes how Israel's Exodus set them apart from all other nations, ancient peoples, and pagan worldviews:

> *[The Exodus] revealed that God was free. He was not limited by either the political or military might of Egypt, however oppressive or brutal. Nor was God limited by historical factors, oppressive armies, or insurmountable natural obstacles, such as the Red Sea. God was not part of the cosmic machine. He was free, and He wanted His children to be free like Him.*
>
> *Oppression and slavery were evils to be routed. They were evil because they were contrary to all that God had intended for the human beings made in His own image. ... Biblical cultures highly value freedom as the essence of God and of His image – humanity* (p. 337).

Or as Wayne Grudem states:

> *When human beings are deprived of their ability to make free choices by evil governments or by other circumstances, a significant part of their God-likeness is suppressed. It is not surprising that they will pay almost any price to regain their freedom. American revolutionary Patrick Henry's cry, 'Give me liberty or give me death!' finds an echo deep within every soul created in the image of God.*[10]

---

[9] pp. 150-51, *A World Without Tyranny.*
[10] pp. 217-18, *Systematic Theology.*

Even secular voices recognize this truth. During the 2020 Covid lockdowns, Jeffrey Tucker rightly predicted:

> *...Human beings will not be forced [forever] to live in cages and think only what our masters tell us to think. We are wired to be free, creative, and truth telling, and cannot abide by systems that attempt to stamp out all those instincts and instead treat us all like lab rats.... No, never.*
>
> *The crazy rules and practices governments and corporations adopted and imposed over the last 20 months will in time, look ridiculous and embarrassing to nearly everyone. That we went along with such preposterous practices is a sad commentary on the human condition and its primitive ways.*[11]

Forgetting God, Forfeiting Freedom

Yet such observers are still limited by their secular, naturalistic worldview. What they fail to see is the spiritual root problem beneath all these bad fruits. "The fool says in his heart, 'There is no God.'", declares Psalm 14. Folly is always self-destructive, as Proverbs often describes (e.g., Prov. 13:20; 15:32; 18:7,9). *Once you deny who God is, you deny who man is* as His image-bearer.

Why then fight for human freedom if there's nothing unique about being human? If there's nothing sacred about human life, why should we not all be miserable slaves? *Everything starts with our view of God.* Psalm 36, "In Your light we see light". "God is light, in Him there is no darkness at all" (1 Jn. 1:5). But outside of God we find darkness – spiritually, morally and in every way.

Aleksandr Solzhenitsyn was perhaps the greatest defender of freedom in the 20th century, exposing the West to the evils of Soviet

---

[11] https://brownstone.org/articles/the-war-weve-lived-and-the-birth-of-the-new/.

Communism (where he spent 8 years in their Gulag prison camps). Solzhenitsyn said:

More than half a century ago, while I was still a child, I recall hearing a number of older people offer the following explanation for the great disasters that had befallen Russia: Men have forgotten God; that's why all this has happened.

Since then I have spent well-nigh fifty years working on the history of our Revolution; in the process I have read hundreds of books, collected hundreds of personal testimonies, and have already contributed eight volumes of my own toward the effort of clearing away the rubble left by that upheaval. But if I were asked today to formulate as concisely as possible the main cause of the ruinous Revolution that swallowed up some sixty million of our people, I could not put it more accurately than to repeat: Men have forgotten God; that's why all this has happened.

What is more, the events of the Russian Revolution can only be understood now, at the end of the century, against the background of what has since occurred in the rest of the world. What emerges here is a process of universal significance. And if I were called upon to identify briefly the principal trait of the entire twentieth century, here too, I would be unable to find anything more precise and pithy than to repeat once again: Men have forgotten God.[12]

Nations that remember God are free; nations that forget God are shackled and bound. "Only those who face up toward God can face down tyrants".[13] Fascism and dictatorships always seem far-fetched at first, until you're in the middle of it, and then it's too late. It's called incrementalism, the 'frog in the kettle' syndrome, slowly and imperceptibly raising the temperature.

---

[12] https://www.pravoslavie.ru/47643.html.
[13] https://dougwils.com/books-and-culture/s7-engaging-the-culture/aphorisms-on-liberty.html.

As de Tocqueville warned Americans nearly 200 years ago, "Despotism may be able to do without faith, but freedom cannot. ...When a people's religion is destroyed...then not only will they let their freedom be taken from them, but often they actually *hand it over themselves*."[14] By design, we are made to be worshippers; if we don't worship God, the state will replace Him as the next most powerful alternative.

As Charlie Kirk has said:

> *Freedom is not a gift from government, freedom is a gift from God.*
>
> *Our rights and liberties don't come from Congress, or Maxine Waters, or Tony Fauci, or any power-hungry DC bureaucrat. Any debate in Congress about when we'll be 'allowed to have our liberties back' means nothing when you know our liberties come from God, not government.*[15]

Freedom At What Price?

What price do you put on human liberty for the glory of God and good of your neighbour? The most blessed, prosperous, and generous nation history has ever known was birthed through the bravery of Christian men like Patrick Henry. It was 23 March, 1775, when this godly patriot and statesman closed his stirring speech to the Continental Congress with these words: "Is life so dear, or peace so sweet, as to be purchased at the price of chains and slavery? Forbid it, Almighty God! I know not what course others may take; but as for me, give me liberty or give me death!"[16]

---

[14] https://xroads.virginia.edu/~Hyper/DETOC/1_ch17.htm.
[15] From Twitter:
https://x.com/charliekirk11/status/1382771178654244865;
https://x.com/charliekirk11/status/827221276368347136.
[16] https://www.colonialwilliamsburg.org/learn/deep-dives/give-me-liberty-or-give-me-death/.

Or as Thomas Paine would eloquently put it one year later (in 1776), "These are the times that try men's souls. The summer soldier and the sunshine patriot will, in this crisis, shrink from the service of his country; but he that stands it now, deserves the love and thanks of man and woman."

Yet our society today asks: 'Is freedom worth dying for? Why all the fuss about tyranny and totalitarianism?' Even Christians say, 'This all sounds so American. Shouldn't the Church just focus on the gospel and not worry about our freedoms? Has the pulpit now become politicised?'

Statues of Liberty

It was France that gave to the USA our 92-metre tall (30-story), 220-ton Statue of Liberty in gratitude for the global reach of freedom, with the famous plaque from poet Emma Lazarus (a Jew) that reads:

Give me your tired, your poor,
Your huddled masses yearning to breathe free,
The wretched refuse of your teeming shore.
Send these, the homeless, tempest-tossed to me,
I lift my lamp beside the golden door!

In South Africa, we have a smaller monument that also makes a loud statement about freedom: the Huguenot monument in Franschhoek, one of my favourite spots to visit (see pic on facing page). It was built to commemorate those stalwart French Protestants who fled persecution and tyranny. South Africa would not be what it is today without their contributions.

At the centre of this monument is a large marble statue of a woman atop a globe of the world. She wears no crown, for she is neither a queen or a goddess; she represents all humanity. In her right hand, she carries a broken chain, depicting freedom from bondage. In her left hand, she holds a Bible, the source of all freedom.

Behind her stand three very tall, white arches symbolising the triune God of our Christian faith, crowned at the top with a cross, symbolising the greatest liberation ever at Calvary. What a privilege for us to stand with this unnamed brave woman, with our Huguenot forefathers in the faith, and in a long line of godly defenders of human dignity and liberty.

Rightly do we sing our South African national anthem, originally a Xhosa Christian revival hymn:[17]

> *Sound the call to come together*
> *And united we shall stand.*
> *Let us live and strive for freedom*
> *In South Africa our land!*

But do we mean those words, or is it just for a good feeling before the kick-off of a soccer or rugby match? Should Christians also (or especially) sing those words; and if so, why?

Vanishing Freedoms

During the 2020 Covid lockdowns, we were eyewitnesses to more attacks on freedom than the world has seen since Hitler and the Nazi Holocaust 80 years ago.[18] I agree with Dr. MacArthur and the pastoral staff at Grace Community Church who stated:

> *We are convinced that governmental encroachment on basic human freedoms constitutes a more intimidating threat to individuals, a greater impediment to the work of the church, and a larger calamity for all of society than any pestilence or other natural disaster. These are difficult times, calling for a thoughtful, biblical, and wise response from church leaders and their congregations.*[19]

---

[17] Here are two articles I've written on this anthem's significance for our Christian witness in South Africa, and in light of our apartheid history:
https://betweentwocultures.com/2023/10/20/let-us-live-and-strive-for-freedom/
https://betweentwocultures.com/2025/07/10/reading-the-ancs-bible-a-christian-response-to-the-freedom-charter/.
[18] My sermons originally for my own flock in Johannesburg have been put into a book recounting our church's stand against oppressive lockdowns, holding underground church services, and suing the government for our religious liberties: *Resisting Tyranny* (Kress Publ., 2022).
[19] https://www.gracechurch.org/news/posts/2254.

Faithful Canadian pastors James Coates and Tim Stephens (both jailed in 2021 for holding church) have warned us already:

> ...Unless the tide of totalitarianism is stemmed, Christians can expect persecution to increase. We've seen that the new prevailing worldview is totalitarian, seeking to define marriage, sexuality, and control health choices. It is absolutely intolerant to opposing beliefs. All socialistic and communistic movements hate the authority and law of God that Christianity promotes.
>
> Much of the Church in Canada believes that compliance and compromise will promote peace and freedom, but this attitude only feeds the beast and will increase persecution and eliminate freedom. ...I anticipate further exile and punishment for non-conformists and those who will still stand and preach truth and reality in our time.[20]

Pastoral Duty

My job as a pastor is to "equip the saints" for serving Christ, which includes teaching them how to "love their neighbour", how to be "salt", "light", and "leaven" in society, "zealous for good works" (Matt. 5:13-16; 7:12; 13:33; 22:39; Tit. 2:14; 3:14). If the local church is to be "the pillar and support of the truth", centred on gospel proclamation, that includes *gospel application* to ethics and daily life (1 Tim. 3:15).

Preaching "the whole counsel of God" means not shrinking back from wherever God's Word must be applied to the issues of the day, proving the authority and sufficiency of Scripture for "training in righteousness", equipping believers to stand up for what is right in every realm of life (Acts 20:27; 2 Tim. 3:16-17). Whenever the church has shone the brightest, she has always had a prophetic voice into society, calling the "kings of the earth" to take heed and hear the word of the Lord (Ps. 2; Jer. 22:29, etc.).

---

[20] https://www.foxnews.com/world/thousands-churches-raise-alarm-scope-new-canadian-conversion-therapy-ban.

Pastoral Compromise

Yet I am baffled and dismayed at how my generation of Christians and church leaders, in the name of being 'gospel-centred', has embraced worldly, secular, leftist attitudes that are more Marxist than Christian, that are anti-freedom, anti-patriotism, anti-human-dignity, and unethical altogether.

We've become like a spoiled kid, fat and lazy from enjoying our blood-bought freedoms for so long; unwilling to pay a price to preserve them for future generations. Yet we're more than happy to emigrate to free countries to enjoy all those freedoms achieved and defended by others?

As Canadian pastor, Jacob Reaume, writes:

> *As we reflect on Kirk's assassination and martyrdom, we should reflect on how Christian leaders and institutions reacted to George Floyd's death five years ago, along with the BLM protests that ensued. George Floyd was a drug addict and violent thief, constantly on the wrong side of the law, and BLM has since been exposed as a Marxist front group run by greedy race-baiting hucksters.*
>
> *Remember the Christian leaders who took to the streets, while they hypocritically were silent about churches remaining locked down by force of law? Remember when they demanded that black squares be displayed on social media to publicly canonize Floyd? Remember when they badgered those who dared question the frenzy? Do you think they will offer a fraction of the same honour to Charlie Kirk, an actual Christian martyr?*
>
> *Does the life of a Christian father, husband, and spokesman matter at least as much as the life of a savage criminal fentanyl addict? The social media records of Christian institutions,*

pastors, and leaders will soon tell. By their fruit you will know them.[21]

Mission of the Church

Dear reader, please understand: This is a call for responsible Christian citizenship, not for politicizing churches. Defending civil freedoms or humanitarian concerns *has never been and cannot become* the mission of a biblical church, or the message of our gospel, as we remain fixed on preaching "Christ and Him crucified" (1 Cor. 2:2; Col. 1:28-29; Rom. 1:16-17). As MacArthur states:

> *Christ and Caesar do operate in different realms. The church's mission is not a partisan political one. There is no political solution to what ails our culture. The church's mission is to preach the gospel, recover souls from the domain of darkness, and train them to be Christ's disciples. Christians must not be dissuaded from that task in order to achieve a mere temporal political objective.*[22]

But upholding human dignity and freedom has always been *the fruit of the church and the result of the gospel's spread.* As the message of the cross powerfully saves souls from the tyranny of sin, it transforms lives, homes and society, so that believers use their God-given freedom to be the best of citizens, finest of neighbours, and most honest and hard-working employees ("seeking the good of the city" in a pagan land, Jer. 29:4-7).

Christians must remember that freedom comes from God and oppression is an evil to be resisted as we diligently pray for our rulers "that we may lead a tranquil and quiet life in all godliness and dignity" (1 Tim. 2:1-4).

---

[21] https://trinitybiblechapel.ca/charlie-kirk-christian-martyr/.
[22] https://www.gty.org/blogs/B220906/why-i-signed-the-frankfurt-declaration.

(2) Freedom is Defined by God's Word

"Freedom is not sustainable if you remove Christianity," proclaimed Charlie Kirk.[23] Curry states, "There is a direct relationship between biblical faith and democratic government, between Judeo-Christianity and human liberty."[24]

Obedient Freedom

Look back at Genesis, as Moses now zooms in on God's creation and command of man on Day 6:

> *The LORD God took the man and put him in the garden of Eden to work it and keep it. And the LORD God commanded the man, saying, "You may surely eat of every tree of the garden, but of the tree of the knowledge of good and evil you shall not eat, for in the day that you eat of it you shall surely die." ...And the man and his wife were both naked and were not ashamed* (vv. 15-17, 25).

Adam and Eve were perfectly and joyfully free – emancipated to live all of life in obedience to their King, following His good and wise commands. Even before the Fall, human freedom was found in God's Word alone.[25] Inside God's revealed, stated boundaries, mankind was free, blessed and prosperous. Outside of God's Law was only cursing, bondage and death. That was the great lie of Satan: "you shall be like God", finding freedom outside of obedience to His Word (Gen. 3:1-7). No wonder the entire Psalter begins as it does, 'How blessed is the man who does not walk…stand…sit with sinners. But his delight is in the

---

[23] https://humanevents.com/2023/04/25/charlie-kirk-to-kirk-cameron-christianity-is-necessary-for-freedom?utm_source=chatgpt.com.
[24] p. 147, *A World Without Tyranny*.
[25] "If we take the cultural mandate seriously, we understand that it necessitates liberty: economic liberty, political liberty, and religious liberty." https://pandrewsandlin.substack.com/p/creational-economics.

law of the LORD..., whatever he does prospers. Not so the wicked...the way of the wicked will perish' (Psalm 1). Twice in the Book of James, God's Word is called, "the law of liberty", because *this Book liberates like no other book!*

It is God's truth that spiritually transforms and unshackles you from sin's bondage. Who then in society should be bigger champions of human liberty, if not us, the people of the Book, whose entire faith is built upon this "royal" and "perfect law of liberty"?

Freed to Obey

Watch for this theme throughout Scripture, throughout history, and throughout your life: Obedience liberates; disobedience enslaves. Walking God's way brings freedom; walking any other way brings bondage. "I shall run the way of Your commandments, For You will enlarge my heart" (Ps. 119:32).

Why did God tell Moses to lead His people out of bondage in Egypt? "Tell Pharoah, 'Let My people go, *so that* they may serve Me" (Exod. 8:1; 9:1). On what basis did God give Israel His Ten Commandments? "I am the LORD your God, who brought you out of the land of Egypt, out of the house of slavery. You shall (x10)...." (Exod. 20). In other words, the Lord was saying, 'I am your King because I am your Redeemer. I freed you so that you will obey Me. You are redeemed for holiness, liberated for the sake of godliness.'

Otherwise, the Israelites would've just gone right back to their old ways as slaves for 400 years in Egypt; they'd just replace Egyptian tyrants with Hebrew ones. *'You can take the slave out of Egypt easier than you can take Egypt out of the slave.'* [26]

---

[26] Os Guiness argues that "the story of Exodus is the highest, richest, and deepest vision for freedom in human history. It serves as the master story of human freedom and provides the greatest sustained critique of the abuse of power." Drawing on the Hebrew and Christian Scriptures, Guinness develops Exodus as the "Magna Carta of humanity, with a constructive vision of a morally responsible society of independent

A God-Centred Freedom

Want proof of how central God's Law was to defining human freedom? Those two tablets with His Ten Commandments (the summary of His entire Law) were written by "His own finger" (Exod. 31:18; Deut. 9:10). They were placed in the Ark of the Covenant and kept inside the tabernacle, inside the very Holy of Holies, under the mercy seat – all this at the centre of their nation wherever they went. God gave His people this constant, visual reminder that durable, lasting freedom is possibly only under the rule of God and the rule of His Law.

In the first place, why did Pharoah even care if the Jews just went away for a few days for a brief worship getaway in the desert? Because Pharoah knew what freedom meant; this pagan king knew more than some pastors today: "Pharaoh instinctively knew that if Israel was set free to worship God, they would never be slaves again. True worship of the living God sets the captives free."[27]

Everything starts with worship. "The fear of the LORD is the beginning of wisdom" and "of understanding" (Prov. 1:7; 9:10). Preserving freedom starts with religious liberty – the freedom to gather and worship the Source and Author of all freedom, the one true and living God.

An Ordered Liberty

In the New Testament, God's Word continues to define freedom further: "having been freed from sin, you became slaves of righteousness. ...For the law of the Spirit of life in Christ Jesus has set you free from the law of sin and death", so that we might obey God's Law and walk in His Spirit, not in the flesh (Rom. 6:17; 8:2-4). The

---

free people who are covenanted to each other and to justice, peace, stability, and the common good of the community – a model from the past that charts our path to the future." *The Magna Carta of Humanity: Sinai's Revolutionary Faith and the Future of Freedom* (2021, IVP).
[27] Toby Sumpter (https://www.christkirk.com/sermon/christian-basis-for-freedom/).

fact is that everyone is a slave; the only question is *whose slave are you?* Do you belong to sin's cruel mastery, or are you subject to Christ's gracious lordship, under His easy yoke (Matt. 11:28-30)?

America's founding fathers, in separating from the tyranny of King George III in England, made clear that this hard-won freedom was not a freedom for selfishness; it was an "ordered liberty", a lawful freedom under the authority of the Creator, King and Judge, the One to Whom we will answer for how we've stewarded these freedoms entrusted to us.

Os Guinness argues that today we face a fundamental crisis of freedom, as "America's genius for freedom has become her Achilles' heel." Our society's conflicts are rooted in "two rival views of freedom, one embodied in 1776 and the ideals of the American Revolution and the other in 1789 and the ideals of the French Revolution."[28] Ideas have consequences.

Paul further declares freedom's purpose in Galatians 5, "It was for freedom that Christ set us free; therefore, keep standing firm and do not be subject again to a yoke of slavery... For you were called to freedom brethren; only do not turn your freedom into an opportunity for the flesh, but through love serve one another" (vv. 1,13). Or as Peter succinctly states, "Act as free men, and do not use your freedom as a covering for evil, but us it as bondslaves of God" (1 Pet. 2:17).

As the Puritan Samuel Bolton wrote in his classic work, *The True Bounds of Christian Freedom*:

> *If Christ has freed us from the penalties, how ought we to subject ourselves to the precepts! If He has delivered us from the curses, how ought we to study the commands! If He paid our debt of sin, certainly we owe a debt of service.*

---

[28] *Last Call for Liberty: How America's Genius for Freedom Has Become Its Greatest Threat* (2018, IVP).

Free Indeed

"Freedom" is a battle cry for the Christian. Yet we must all beware, especially in these days of rising tyranny: If "freedom!" becomes our only watchword (our one-string guitar, the only drum we beat), detached from faith, love and obedience, or cut off from Christ and His cross, then we will be the next casualty in a long line of antinomian, lawless believers. Paul repeatedly warns us against selfishly abusing our liberties at the expense of others (1 Cor. 8-10; Rom. 14).

Jesus Himself put it most boldly, in light of the worst bondage of all, the captivity behind all other captivities: "Truly, truly I say to you, everyone who commits sin is a slave to sin. ...If the Son makes you free, you will be free indeed" (Jn. 8:34,36). As Charles Wesley testified of his own conversion:

> *Long my imprisoned spirit lay*
> *Fast bound in sin and nature's night;*
> *Thine eye diffused a quickening ray,*
> *I woke, the dungeon flamed with light;*
> *My chains fell off, my heart was free,*
> *I rose, went forth, and followed Thee!*

It is imperative that we define freedom correctly. Our society uses the same word but smuggles in a new definition. God says "freedom" is about obeying Him; our world says, "freedom" is about satisfying self, as long as you don't 'harm anyone else'. These are polar opposite definitions. Scripture does not teach a freedom that exalts *personal autonomy* as the highest good; it says *personal virtue* and duty are the highest good. *Liberty is not to do as I please, but to do as God pleases.*

False Freedoms

We live in a culture drowning in false freedom, thanks especially to Hollywood. For example, consider the demonic, false doctrines of

Disney: "No right, no wrong, no rules for me I'm free. Let it go, let it go!" (from the movie, *Frozen*).

The culture says freedom means: 'freedom of choice' to murder unborn babies; 'freedom of expression' to pursue every form of pornographic perversion and sexual immorality; 'freedom to marry' the same gender; 'freedom of identity' to indoctrinate children with LGBTQ lies, to restrict free speech, to cancel all dissent. Yet all these abuses of freedom should not silence Christians; it should make us even more vocal in defending true human freedom.

John Adams (2nd president of USA) once warned: "Our Constitution was made only for a moral and religious people. It is wholly inadequate to the government of any other."[29] Or as another historian warned in 1805:

> *If this (bondage) should ever become the deplorable situation of the United States, let some unborn historian in a far distant day, detail the lapse, and hold up the contrast between a simple, virtuous, and free people, and a degenerate, servile race of beings, corrupted by wealth, effeminated by luxury, impoverished by licentiousness, and become the automatons of intoxicated ambition.*[30]

May God preserve us from this fate by reviving His Church and restoring us to an ordered liberty.[31]

---

[29] https://founders.archives.gov/documents/Adams/99-02-02-3102.
[30] https://theimaginativeconservative.org/2021/10/essence-freedom-bradley-birzer.html.
[31] My friend, Pastor David De Bruyn, has written a superb biblical theology of freedom in his recent book, *The War on Words*, Chapter 6, with many wise clarifications and applications to the Christian life and churches. Also found here:
https://religiousaffections.org/articles/articles-on-culture/freedom/
https://religiousaffections.org/articles/articles-on-culture/freedom-societal-and-individual/
https://religiousaffections.org/articles/articles-on-culture/freedom-and-churches/

(3) Freedom is a Treasure

Miguel de Cervantes (author of *Don Quixote*) famously said:

> *Liberty is one of the choicest gifts that Heaven hath bestowed upon man and exceeds in volume all the treasures which the earth contains within its bosom.... Liberty, as well as honor, man ought to preserve at the hazard of his life, for without it, life is insupportable.*[32]

Benjamin Franklin rightly warned, "Those who would give up essential liberty to purchase a little temporary safety, deserve neither liberty nor safety."[33] From painful experience and careful study, he knew what few today seem to recognise – freedom's inestimable value.

How God Views Bondage

Why did God appear at the burning bush and send Moses to rescue the Israelites? Yes, it was supremely for His glory and His great redemption plan; but He also makes clear it was His compassion for His captive people in their misery: "I have surely seen the affliction of My people who are in Egypt, and have given heed to their cry because of their taskmasters, for I am aware of their sufferings" (Exod. 3:7). There was nothing desirable about human bondage.

In the Bible, slavery to tyrants is always a curse, never a blessing. Oppression signifies God's judgment, never His favour. The whole Book of Judges tells the story of repeated cycles of God's discipline

---

https://religiousaffections.org/articles/articles-on-culture/matters-of-conscience-and-freedom/
https://religiousaffections.org/articles/articles-on-church/judging-matters-of-freedom/.
[32] https://www.gutenberg.org/cache/epub/996/pg996-images.html.
[33] https://oll.libertyfund.org/quote/benjamin-franklin-on-the-trade-off-between-essential-liberty-and-temporary-safety-1775.

upon His wayward people, handing them over to tyrants. Idolatry always brings bondage. Yet God hears the cries of the oppressed and delivers.

What is one of the most beloved Old Testament images for prizing human freedom? It is the glad prospect of "every man under his own vine and under his own fig tree" (1 Kgs 4:25; 2 Kgs 18:31; Isa. 36:16; Micah 4:4). The vine and the fig tree are means of sustenance, objects of ownership and work, signifying peace, prosperity – the blessings of liberty.

Human Responsibility

Personhood for us, as God's image-bearers, means choosing between right and wrong. "I have set before you life and death, blessing and curse. Therefore choose life!" (Deut. 30:19). "Choose you this day whom you will serve!" (Josh 24:15). Often our Lord Jesus invited people, 'Come to Me, Take and eat, Follow Me, Listen to Me!' (Matt. 11:28; Rev. 22:17, etc.). Our biblical convictions about the bondage of the will should underline human responsibility and dignity, not negate it.[34]

The Jubilee

Why did the prophets declare that Messiah would come? Isaiah makes clear (the first text Jesus' read aloud in the synagogue at outset of His public ministry): "The Spirit of the LORD is upon Me to...proclaim liberty/release to the captives...to set free those who are oppressed" (Isa. 61:1; Lk. 4:18). True, that promise is *not* about political, earthly freedom (we reject all forms of Liberation Theology). It is entirely about spiritual liberty of the heart from sin and guilt. Yet the obvious assumption is that liberty is good, slavery is bad.

---

[34] https://www.gotquestions.org/free-will.html.

When a desperate, impoverished Jew would sell themselves into slavery, what provision did our merciful God make? On both the 7th year and the 50th, they were liberated (Deut. 15:15; Lev. 25:42. For this reason, God called for the Jubilee declaration: "Proclaim liberty throughout all the land!" (Lev. 25:10). Those are the biblical words engraved on America's famous Liberty Bell in Philadelphia (see pic on inside page before Introduction on p. 7).

Defending Tyranny?

God outlawed all forms of slavery: "He who kidnaps a man, whether he sells him or he is found in his possession, shall surely be put to death" (Exod. 21:16). That meant stealing another person's autonomy/freedom through forcible enslavement was prohibited. The New Testament teaches the same, that it is against God's law to be a "slave-trader, man-stealer, kidnapper" (1 Tim. 1:10).

Likewise, Paul wrote to converted slaves, "If you are able to become free, do that. You were bought with a price [Christ's own blood]; do not become slaves of men" (1 Cor. 7:21ff). God's Word never romanticises or minimises human slavery. How then, in the name of being 'gospel-centred', did it become a virtue to speak out against human freedom and in defence of tyranny?

Giving Up Which Freedoms?

In 2020, we heard countless Christian leaders saying, 'Lockdowns, church bans, mask and vaccine mandates, these are all great opportunities to love our neighbour by *giving up our freedoms,* sacrificing our liberties for the greater good.' But no matter how nice and spiritual that sounds at first, it is a half-truth and a twisting of Scripture. Paul speaks about giving up personal opinions and religious preferences for the sake of the weaker brother, lest he violate his own conscience and injure his faith (1 Cor. 8-10; Rom. 14).

But that is not the same as giving up hard-won civic freedoms and the public good of my neighbour and of all society to become a doormat to dictators. There is nothing Christian about throwing away the cherished liberties we enjoy in the West that were birthed out of a biblical worldview.

Unlike in Bible times, we're reaping the rich fruits of centuries of Christian influence, for which we should be profoundly thankful, not cavalier and dismissive. For the love of God and country, my grandfather and my father bravely fought and risked their lives for freedom and against tyranny.

I'm grateful for holidays that remind us of this, like Memorial Day and Veteran's Day, "lest we forget". I gladly sing with my family patriotic hymns rooted in biblical truth, such as Samuel Smith's great anthem:

My country, 'tis of thee,
Sweet land of liberty,
Of thee I sing;
Land where my fathers died,
Land of the pilgrims' pride,
From ev'ry mountainside
Let freedom ring!

Our fathers' God to Thee,
Author of liberty,
To Thee we sing.
Long may our land be bright,
With freedom's holy light,
Protect us by Thy might,
Great God our King.[35]

---

[35] Historically, hymnals have had a closing section of hymns (not only in America) entitled, "National", "The Nation", "Family & Nation", or "Patriotic". Strangely, that section has vanished from most modern hymnals. Another indication of our pietistic captivity?

True Neighbour-Love

In our church, we have numerous men who bravely served in our South African military service during the Border War of the 1970s and 80s against communism, securing freedoms we still enjoy today because of their sacrifice. Even if the enemy was mislabelled 'die swaart gevaar' ('the black danger') by a racist, apartheid government, 'die rooi gevaar' ('the red danger' of communism) was a true enemy and is today a greater threat to our world perhaps than ever before. I thank God for these valiant men who defended our treasured liberties.

It is also an unbiblical redefining of love to suggest that we give up human rights in the name of Christian love. Says one pastor:

> *If we turn our heads or act with indifference when our neighbours are covered with the weight of tyranny or injustice, we are in fact hating our neighbours. If I am not jealous for their liberty, their freedom and protection, I hate my neighbour. Love for neighbour demands that we resist tyranny as an act of obedience to God.*[36]

C.S. Lewis spoke clearly of that noble "love of country", a lost virtue in our individualistic and cynical age. Speaking of patriotism, Lewis asks, "Who can condemn what clearly makes many people, at many important moments, behave so much better than they could have done without its help?"[37] Yet I sadly hear evangelical leaders today disparagingly speak about politically conservative Christians as those old-fashioned and out-dated, "God-and-country believers".

---

[36] From Jeff Durbin at Apologia Church in Phoenix, AZ. Or as D. Curry states, "The biblical injunction that we love our neighbor means that we cannot ignore modern tyranny" (p. 143, *A World Without Tyranny*).
[37] https://www.cslewisinstitute.org/Reflections_Patriotism;
https://www.cslewis.com/the-practical-side-of-lewis-patriotism/;
https://www.religiousfreedominstitute.org/blog/cs-lewis-on-love-of-country-and-love-of-god-an-independence-day-reflection.

Upholding Human Freedom

The 8th Commandment is yet another biblical proof of God's commitment to human freedom: "You shall not steal" (Exod. 20:15; Deut. 5:19). Unlike Karl Marx (and socialists and communists), God believes in private property rights – in your freedom to earn, acquire and own. God and His prophets rebuke state thieves who trample on human freedom – such as King David taking another man's wife, or King Ahab stealing Naboth's vineyard (2 Sam. 11-12; 1 Kgs 21).

Grudem concludes:

Throughout the Bible, from the beginning of Genesis to the last chapter of Revelation, God honors and protects human freedom and human choice. Liberty is an essential component of our humanity. Any government that significantly denies people's liberty exerts a terribly dehumanizing influence on its people.[38]

Remember the awful cry of the unvaccinated captives in 2020: "Hi, I'm a Canadian citizen. I haven't broken any laws, but I can't work, can't go to a restaurant/movie theatre, can't ski, can't take my kid to swimming or soccer; cannot leave my country, or fly within it, nor board a train or a ship. SOS!"[39]

This writer captures well freedom's priceless value:

Freedom matters—even in a pandemic. Without freedom, elderly people may spend their remaining time on earth isolated from their loved ones, and we know that social isolation kills. Without

---

[38] p. 92, *Politics According to the Bible*. Grudem also updates, develops and applies these arguments further in his superb book, *The Poverty of Nations: A Sustainable Solution* (2013, Crossway). Based on biblical principle and specific examples, Grudem spells out 21 different freedoms government should protect for a nation to prosper (pp. 259-307).
[39] https://x.com/truthwins_/status/1452477298414800904.

freedom, people may lose not only their livelihoods but the momentum and opportunity to build careers as flight attendants, orchestra musicians, chefs, or scientists working on viruses. Without freedom, children may lose important and irretrievable experiences and milestones. Without freedom, life becomes a shadow of itself.[40]

Inner & Outer Freedom

Dear friends, there is a badly forgotten, much-needed truth in our day— *inner freedom leads to outer freedom*. Spiritual liberation cannot stay there; it spills over into all of life. This is the story of the past 2,000 years, wherever the Bible has gone. This treasure of liberty has been Christianity's gift to the world!

British historian, Paul Johnson, wrote:

> *[Spiritual freedom in Christ] is the father of all other freedoms. For conscience is the enemy of tyranny and the compulsory society [that coerces].... The notions of political and economic freedom both spring from the Christian conscience as a historic force.*[41]

Puritan Thomas Brooks wrote, "What goes from a people when the gospel goes? Answer: peace, prosperity, safety, civil liberty, true glory, and soul-happiness, the presence of God (2 Chron. 13:9; 15:3, 5, 6; 1 Sam. 4:22; Jer. 2:11-13)".[42]

Curry reminds us:

> *Throughout the long centuries of history, the twin tyrannies of oppression and poverty have been a normal part of the human experience. Just 300 years ago famines ravaged the world every generation, plagues were a regular occurrence, life expectancy in*

---

[40] https://brownstone.org/articles/the-freedumb-fallacy/.
[41] p. 516, *A History of Christianity*.
[42] p. 9, *Smooth Stones from Ancient Brooks*.

many countries was below thirty, there were no effective medicines, most people were illiterate, infant mortality rates exceeded 50 percent, and the average person spent most, if not all, that he had to provide food and shelter for himself and his family.

Moreover, nearly all individuals lived their lives unprotected from the capricious acts of despotic rulers. Respect for the dignity and inviolability of human beings was – with the exception of England, and there only partially – institutionalized nowhere. The rule of law was arbitrary and often non-existent. The concept of human rights was virtually unknown.[43]

19th-century poet, James Russel Lowell, stated:

I challenge any sceptic to find a 10-square mile spot on this planet where they can live their lives in peace and safety and decency, where womanhood is honoured, where infancy and old age are revered, where they can educate their children, where the Gospel of Jesus Christ has not gone first to prepare the way. If they find such a place, then I would encourage them to emigrate [there] and proclaim their unbelief.[44]

Freedom as Fruit of the Gospel

Mangalwadi writes of William Carey's missionary legacy, "India's freedom was a fruit of the gospel. ...Without the Bible's political ideas, Muslim emperors, Hindu militia, or European merchants would still be ruling India".[45] He contrasts this to the unbiblical, bloody freedoms trumpeted by the French Revolution:

Without the Bible, democracy became what Plato had condemned as the worst of all political systems. ...America, not France, became the beacon of liberty, precisely because it allowed the Bible to shape

---

[43] pp. 143-44, *A World Without Tyranny*.
[44] p. 330 in D. Noebel, *Understanding the Times*.
[45] p. 351, *The Book That Made Your World*.

its cultural ethos. ...Only cultures founded on the Bible have viewed freedom as a virtue worth dying for. ...[As another historian observes] *It is impossible to enslave mentally or socially a Bible-reading people.*⁴⁶

As de Tocqueville famously stated in his classic, *Democracy in America*, "Despotism may be able to do without faith, but freedom cannot."

The Best Friend of Slaves

Here in South Africa, when was slavery finally abolished? In 1833, because of that heroic defender of freedom in England, Christian politician William Wilberforce. And 150 years later, what brought the end of the evils of Apartheid here in this land? Once again, significant Christian influence and prayer played a vital role.⁴⁷

During the American Civil War, it was an abolitionist hymnwriter, in defending the civil rights of black slaves and upholding human liberty and equality, who wrote "The Battle Hymn of the Republic":

As Christ died to make men holy,
Let us die to make men free.

This divine gift of human freedom cannot be kept to ourselves. At the University of Stellenbosch in the 1990s, Wynoma Michaels was a PhD student and the first black woman to be student president. She said, "although the Bible was abused, nothing else gave my people a greater sense of their own worth and meaning than the Good Book. It was the

---

⁴⁶ P. 337, ibid
⁴⁷ https://www.jubilee-centre.org/cambridge-papers/peacebuilding-ending-apartheid-jeremy-ive; https://www.amazon.com/Footprints-African-Sand-Life-Times-ebook/dp/B07NP6TDY5 (Michael Cassidy's autobiography); https://www.christianitytoday.com/ct/1994/august15/4t9019.html; https://www.amazon.com/Story-Church-South-Africa/dp/1839731583/ (Kevin Roy's excellent history of Christianity in S.Africa).

one book the slave-owner and slave shared in common; they both knew they stood under its authority as equals. ...A great number of my people took the trouble to become literate for one supreme reason: To read the Bible."

Mangalwadi adds, "Today the Bible is the chief factor in the opening of the African mind, just as it was the key to opening the Western mind."[48] Who can put a price on this treasure of freedom which God's Word brought to the modern world?

20th century Protestant stalwart and founder of Westminster Seminary, J. Gresham Machen, gets to the root issue when he writes:

> *If liberty is to be preserved against the materialistic paternalism of the modern state, there must be something more than courts and legal guarantees; freedom must be written not merely in the constitution but in the people's heart. And it can be written in the heart, we believe, only as a result of the redeeming work of Christ* (from his *Selected Shorter Writings*).

It was no mystery that Charlie Kirk treasured God's sacred gift of liberty:[49]

> *Patriotism is not blind loyalty to government, but fierce loyalty to the principles that make America great. ...Faith and freedom go hand in hand. A nation that loses its faith will inevitably lose its freedom. ...American exceptionalism is not arrogance; it's gratitude for the unique blessings of liberty.*

Likewise, my wife's grandfather, Dr. Robert L. Gates, faithfully taught American history for 52 years in high school and university classrooms always explaining the uniquely Christian roots of the American idea. May God raise up many more history teachers like him for today's students!

---

[48] p. 354, ibid.
[49] https://rememberingcharliekirk.org/quotes.

(4) Freedom is Fragile

In 1787, when the United States' Constitution was drafted, a lady asked Ben Franklin what the founders had given the American people. "A republic," he retorted, "if you can keep it."[50] It is not enough for freedom to be won. It must also be sustained.

Francis Schaeffer was warning of this in the 20th century: "Culture and the freedoms of people are fragile. Without a sufficient base, when such pressures come, only time is needed – and often not a great deal of time – before there is a collapse."[51] Says Guinness, "In the end, the ultimate threat to the American republic will be Americans. The problem is not wolves at the door but termites in the floor."[52]

One defender of freedom wrote:

> It is the common fate of the indolent to see their rights become a prey to the active. The condition upon which God hath given liberty to man is eternal vigilance; which condition if he break, servitude is at once the consequence of his crime and the punishment of his guilt.[53]

Ronald Reagan stated:

> Freedom is never more than one generation away from extinction. We didn't pass it to our children in the bloodstream. It must be fought for, protected, and handed on for them to do the same, or one day we will spend our sunset years telling our

---

[50] This is the title of Eric Metaxas' important book, *If You Can Keep It: The Forgotten Promise of American Liberty* (2017, Penguin).
[51] p. 87, *How Should We Then Live?* (1976, Crossway).
[52] *A Free People's Suicide: Sustainable Freedom and the American Future* (2012, IVP).
[53] https://pacificlegal.org/eternal-vigilance-the-price-of-freedom/.

*children and our children's children what it was once like...where men were free.*⁵⁴

Albert Mohler gives this pertinent warning in our 21ˢᵗ century:

> *...We're looking at a re-definition of the world order. That's what Vladimir Putin is pushing for. That's what Xi Jinping is pushing for as the dictator of China. ...Western elites, having separated themselves so much from the biblical understanding of sin, vastly over-estimate human goodness. They also vastly over-calculate just how committed other nations are to a certain kind of political agreement.*
>
> *...John Quincy Adam's famously said that Americans "do not go abroad seeking monsters to destroy"; but we do need to understand we live in a world that increasingly is demonstrating the challenge of monsters who would destroy us and would destroy ordered liberty, constitutional government.*⁵⁵

These leaders are stating what the Bible said long ago, from our Lord Himself: "To whom much is given, much will be required" (Luke 12:48). As with all of God's gifts, if we don't steward them wisely, He will take them away. We live in a Romans 1 world of ingratitude and idolatry, "suppressing the truth in unrighteousness", being handed over by God Himself to all kinds of bondage (Rom. 1:18-32).

Recognising Three Spheres

It is because of freedom's fragility that God's Word designates the separate spheres of authority, lest any sphere encroach upon the

---
⁵⁴ https://www.reaganlibrary.gov/archives/speech/january-5-1967-inaugural-address-public-ceremony.
⁵⁵ https://albertmohler.com/2022/02/15/briefing-2-15-22

jurisdiction of another.[56] History is replete with examples of the harm that comes from family dynasty's ruling church or state, or church empires ruling family and state, or today's iron-fisted state trampling over the rights of families and churches.[57]

For this reason the excellent Frankfurt Declaration (of 2022) affirms these three biblical spheres:

> *We affirm that all earthly authorities derive their authority ('the right to be obeyed') from God, who is over all and to whom all must give account. We believe that He has established their different spheres of responsibility (i.e., mandates) and in so doing has set limits to their authority.*
>
> *God has delegated authority to civil governments for the purpose of rewarding good and punishing evil, and to protect the God-given rights and freedoms granted to all people.*
>
> *He has also delegated authority to the Church in its various expressions, particularly to make disciples of all nations by preaching the Word of God, and to establish and administer redeemed communities of faith living under the authority of Christ.*
>
> *In addition, He has delegated authority to the family as the basic unit of society for the purpose of fostering societal cohesion and sexual fidelity, and to protect, provide for, raise, and educate children in the way of the Lord. We affirm our right as citizens,*

---

[56] See B. Laird, *Family, Government & Church: Relating Three Jurisdictions of Divinely Delegated Authority* (2021, Shepherd Press).

[57] "We must resist authoritarian impulses and exercises by various officials seeking to consolidate power and impose their will over the constitutional processes and guarantees we enjoy. Our Constitution was designed and ratified for exactly such challenges, and it has endured 231 years through a myriad of challenges far more grave than a virus." https://www.gatestoneinstitute.org/17984/vaccines-and-power

parents, and Christians to freely self-determine our beliefs and behaviors based on these truths.[58]

Stewarding Freedom

Curry writes:

> *A biblically faithful, responsible Christian approach to international politics must start with a sensitivity to the evils of tyranny and an appreciation of the achievements of democratic government. God, through His grace, has given mankind the gift of freedom. It is our Christian responsibility to act as stewards of this gift.*[59]

As another historian rightly sobers us with the ongoing evils of North Korea, as testified by insiders who have escaped:

> *When [we] behave like devotees to bureaucrats and politicians, much can go wrong. North Koreans worship authority. ...to avoid further forfeiture of our liberties, we can recognize the warning signs of where the worship of authority mindset can lead us.*

> *...Today, many [people], including healthcare professionals, stifle their questions because to ask means they can 'no longer exist in their system.' Inquiry is being crushed and freedom is eroding. [This] 'soft' crushing of inquiry is far removed from North Korea's brutal totalitarian dystopia.*

---

[58] https://frankfurtdeclaration.com
[59] p. 152, *A World Without Tyranny*

> *Yet, lessons from North Korea are warning signs. Why would we go further down the path to hell on earth when North Korea is a living example of the mindset that generates such a hell?*[60]

Don't Kid Yourself

Solzhenitsyn often warned the apathetic, complacent free world in the West (looking on at the evils of communism): "There always is this fallacious belief: 'It would not be the same here; here such things are impossible.' Alas, all the evil of the twentieth century is possible everywhere on earth." It is not a virtue to be naïve; the Bible calls us to live soberly and temperately, unsurprised by any extent of human evil and depravity in this fallen world.

Hear this urgent and specific call to preserve our freedoms:

> *At the heart of any free society are institutions that support freedom and protect us from government tendencies toward tyranny. ..."We the People" are responsible for seeing that the government does not begin to serve itself instead of the people who have elected it. So, the people in a free society have a serious obligation to "keep the republic," to paraphrase Ben Franklin. We are responsible for living out our freedoms — and for exercising them.*
>
> *But usually, we do that best through institutions, like universities. ...To the extent universities have surrendered to corrosive* [anti-freedom] *forces and are increasingly unable to countenance ideas or voices or opinions that might push against the increasingly propagandistic shouting of the secular left, we should expect the same fruit as we have seen grow every time this has happened before.*

---

[60] https://www.aier.org/article/worshiping-authority-leads-to-tyranny-five-lessons-from-north-korea/

> *If ideas they consider "conservative" or "faith-based" are categorically and cavalierly demonized as "racist" or "bigoted" and disallowed, truth has already left the building, and murder and general tragedy cannot help but follow. If those of us in universities especially — but everywhere in our culture — do not fight heroically against the culturally Marxist stormtroopers around us, we will certainly not have the opportunity to fight tomorrow.*[61]

This is precisely why Charlie Kirk lived and died proclaiming truth on university campuses. As Dennis Prager lamented after Charlie's death:

> *We have lost the most articulate spokesman for America and its unique value system—a country founded to be free, based on Jerusalem and Athens, the Judeo-Christian value system and the Greek emphasis on logic and reason.*[62]

As society today moves increasingly leftward, inequality is now seen as the greatest threat, not tyranny. Good and evil are replaced by the new 'moral' categories of rich and poor (privileged and under-privileged) as the greater injustice. Thus, the highest goal for society is no longer "liberty and justice for all", and creation of wealth from which all benefit. Instead, the chief aim is material equality and redistribution of wealth. This is the product of Marxist thinking, which has led to tyranny and poverty every single time.[63]

The Washington Post said that believing human freedom is an inalienable right to which all are entitled, "is a key component in White

---

[61] https://www.standingforfreedom.com/2022/01/indoctrination-the-paved-road-to-deceit-and-death/
[62] https://www.prageru.com/remembering-our-dear-friend-charlie-kirk
[63] See Dennis Prager, *Still the Best Hope* (2013, Broadside Books)

supremacy".[64] This is our ignorant, Marxist, anti-freedom world racing towards tyranny and bondage.

Protecting Individuals from the Herd

One historian gives this sobering description of how our liberties are under assault today:

> ...*The great horrors of the 20th century, like Stalin's Holodomor, the Holocaust, and the Khmer Rouge's Cambodian genocide, were all rationalized by their perpetrators as necessary to achieve some alleged greater good. When the inalienable individual rights of the minority conflicted with an alleged greater good for the majority, inalienable rights were swept aside. The end justified the means.*

> ...*Once society allowed the philosophy of utilitarianism to erode the ironclad protection of individual rights and freedoms, it was just a matter of time until some critical emergency would justify sweeping away individual human rights to achieve some alleged greater good.*

> ...*Life, liberty, the pursuit of happiness, property rights, freedom of speech, limits on the power of government, universal human rights, etc., are principles designed to protect the individual from the herd.*

> ...*Pop culture increasingly mirrors and reinforces this shift. Even the current batch of superhero movies reflect this. Most no longer follow the theme of "one against many" but have shifted instead to a team approach to solving problems. The lone warrior has been replaced by the team player. And it is not the individual*

---

[64] https://www.washingtonpost.com/outlook/2022/02/11/ottawa-trucker-convoy-is-rooted-canadas-settler-colonial-history/; https://notthebee.com/article/wapo-the-belief-that-ones-entitled-to-freedom-is-a-key-component-of-white-supremacy-

that requires protection, but rather the entire herd or team because safety lies at the center of the collective, which must pull together for the greater good. We're all supposed to be in this together, so responsibility to protect the individual has been replaced by responsibility to protect the herd.

...Even censorship, propaganda, and radical social engineering all begin to take on a moral veneer when they are justified as being for the good of the herd. The woke culture wars of today and the lockdown/COVID-Zero crowd have the same philosophical impulses as the ambitious social-engineers of the past, like Robespierre, Marx, Engels, Stalin, Hitler, Mao, and Castro, who also had no qualms about sacrificing truth, liberty, and even lives for the alleged good of the herd.[65]

Learn the Difference

One of the keys to Charlie Kirk's prowess in debates was that he was well-grounded and well-read on the stark differences between Classic Liberalism and Illiberal Progressivism, which is the reigning and ruining ideology of our day.

As a true conservative, Charlie could contrast true and false freedom in every category, from: human nature, rights, flourishing, responsibility, conflict, and human potential; to truth claims, morality, religion, private property, social justice, speech, economics, meritocracy, social hierarchies, and armed citizenry; to multiculturalism, national assimilation, sexual ethics, the unborn, transgenderism and marriage.[66]

---

[65] https://www.juliusruechel.com/2021/03/preparing-ground-for-mass-hysteria-what.html
[66] See a superb summary chart here, very helpful:
https://www.brettbonecutter.com/post/the-liberal-legacy-of-charlie-kirk

Indiana Illustration

The more we are convinced of a biblical view of individual, inalienable human rights granted by God, and the more we appreciate our rich and costly heritage of freedom, the more we will hate tyranny and oppose it wherever we can. Even if your resistance looks different than mine. But if we don't treasure God's gift of freedom, there will be little or no resistance at all and freedom will be lost..

Here's a fine example of a Christian defence of civic freedom, from Lafayette, Indiana. Their City Council was proposing to ban all efforts at helping people to live out their God-given gender, something that the Christian gospel is all about - transformed lives (1 Cor. 6:9-11; 2 Cor. 5:17)! Faith Church lead an effort among churches to protest this attack on religious freedom, which would effectively outlaw biblical Christianity altogether. They declared, "The principles of religious freedom and the separation of church and state are cherished ideals which must never be surrendered."[67] They won that battle![68]

Not Escapists

As Christians, we know that Jesus said the world will get worse in these last days before His return (Matt. 24). Countless believers across history and around the world today, like Charlie Kirk, have been imprisoned and martyred for the sake of Christ, with no earthly hope of preserving their freedoms.

Yet they gladly suffered for their Lord, and so must we. During the great 7-year tribulation, by God's own design, Antichrist will brutally trample on every vestige of human rights and freedoms (Rev. 12-13). The world will at last unite under one ruler, and he will be the most evil tyrant history has ever known.

---

[67] https://www.freedomlafayette.org/
[68] https://www.freedomlafayette.org/post/a-big-win-for-the-integrity-of-christian-ministry-and-christian-families

Yet Christ will then come and crush all His foes and usher in His kingdom of perfect righteousness, peace, and freedom. None of these prospects make us escapists in the present age or cancel our duty to love our neighbour and defend human rights wherever we can. We labour this day in light of that day to be found faithful when the King returns.

We need to remember a battle cry and biblical conviction of our Protestant forefathers, "Resistance to tyrants is obedience to God", as illustrated by the Hebrew midwives, Elijah, John the Baptist and our Lord Himself and the apostles (Exod. 1:17; 1 Kgs 18:17; Mk 6:18-29; Matt. 22:21; 26:64). But obedience to tyrants is disobedience to God (Acts 4:19-20; 5:29).[69]

Biting the Hand that Fed Us

It would be foolish and ungrateful for believers not to appreciate all the benefits we've received from these Judeo-Christian ideas and the price paid for these freedoms by our forefathers. Surely part of the Church being "salt and light" in society, and "loving our neighbour as ourselves", would be active participation in a democracy so that we are not responsible for allowing laws that punish good and reward evil to become entrenched (Matt. 5:12-14; 7:12).[70]

God is sovereign and Christ can build His Church under the worst of tyrants and the fiercest of persecution, but that doesn't mean the consequences for the Church, missions, and human dignity in those lands have not been devastating. Nor does it mean that we passively wait for South Africa to become the next North Korea or Venezuela, not doing all that we can to prevent it. It's been rightly said, "All that it takes for evil to triumph is for good men to do nothing."

---

[69] https://www.gracechurch.org/news/posts/2254
[70] Wayne Grudem's fine work, *Politics According to the Bible*, grapples with many such questions.

Praise God for the brave Wilberforces of history, whom God used in their vocation to overturn the global evil of slavery, and the faithful pastors like John Newton who equipped and encouraged Wilberforce to do so. Wilberforce's lifelong prayer was, "May I be the instrument of stopping such a course of wickedness." As was rightly said about Wilberforce, "A private faith that does not act in the face of oppression is no faith at all."[71] Charlie Kirk has surely been a Wilberforce in our day.

Freedom at a Crossroads

The Christian scholar and statesman, Os Guinness (who is British), has written numerous biblical and historical books defending freedom and exhorting the American Church in particular:

> *There are two revolutionary faiths bidding to take the world forward. ...There is no choice facing America and the West that is more urgent and consequential than the choice between Sinai and Paris. Will the coming generation return to faith in God and to humility, or continue to trust in the all-sufficiency of Enlightenment reason, punditry, and technocracy? Will its politics be led by principles or by power? ...We must choose...between faith in God and faith in reason alone, between freedom and despotism, and between life and death.*[72]

As the former Australian Deputy Prime Minister (1999-2005), John Anderson, once stated:

> *It will be a tragedy of inestimable proportions for the American people if that great nation eats its own legendary commitment to freedom from within. Equally, to lose the leadership of the*

---

[71] 71 p. xiii, introduction by C. Colson to Wilberforce's classic, *A Practical View of Christianity*
[72] *The Magna Carta of Humanity: Sinai's Revolutionary Faith and the Future of Freedom* (2021, IVP)

world's most powerful champion of liberty would be truly dangerous for non-Americans everywhere in these increasingly unsettled times.[73]

Power of One

As Charlie Kirk's legacy illustrates, never underestimate the power of one brave voice willing to swim upstream, resolved to live by conviction instead of coercion. We have the Nicene Creed and understand the doctrine of the Trinity today because when Bishop Athanasius was told to back down because the whole world was against him, he stubbornly replied, "Then I am against the world." Don't doubt the impact of one 'Athanasius Contra Mundum' with a Christlike face like flint (Isa. 50:7), determined to stand alone, like Luther against the entire Diet of Worms. *All that it takes for evil to triumph is for good men to do nothing.*

Refuse to live any longer by lies. Choose to live by truth and stand for freedom. Abraham Kuyper, Christian theologian and Prime Minister of the Netherlands (1901-05) said: "In any successful attack on freedom, the state can only be an accomplice. The chief culprit is the citizen who forgets his duty."[74]

Sophie Scholl was a 21-year-old Christian university student executed for leading a peaceful protest against Hitler. These were her last recorded words:

> *How can we expect righteousness to prevail when there is hardly anyone willing to give himself up individually to a righteous cause? Such a fine, sunny day, and I have to go, but what does*

---

[73] In endorsing Os Guinness, *Last Call for Liberty* (2018, IVP)
[74] https://www.cpjustice.org/public/page/content/2017_kuyper_lecture_remarks
Another fine example of standing up for freedom at the local level, a small Christian university taking on the White House: https://adfmedia.org/case/college-ozarks-v-biden

my death matter, if through us, thousands of people are awakened and stirred to action?[75]

How would slavery or apartheid have ever ended if all the Christians, in the name of being 'gospel-centred', just stayed in hiding or submitted to unlawful and evil regulations?

As Martin Niemoller, one of the few brave pastors who confronted Nazi Germany (and was imprisoned), warned:

> *First they came for the socialists, and I did not speak out – because I was not a socialist. Then they came for the trade unionists, and I did not speak out – because I was not a trade unionist. Then they came for the Jews, and I did not speak out – because I was not a Jew. Then they came for me – and there was no one left to speak for me.*[76]

After Charlie Kirk's assassination, Virgil Walker told a group of students at Judson University, "Time is running out, and your generation is the last line of defense between biblical Christianity and total cultural collapse."[77]

Here's how William Wolfe urges us to carry on Charlie's legacy:

> *Christians must drag their convictions into the political fray like never before. We've dawdled too long in our ecclesiastical bunkers, letting secularists warp "church-state separation" into a gag order on the Gospel.*

---

[75] https://historicalsnaps.com/2018/02/11/the-last-words-of-sophie-scholl/; https://www.thegospelcoalition.org/article/75-years-ago-hans-sophie-scholl/
[76] https://encyclopedia.ushmm.org/content/en/article/martin-niemoeller-first-they-came-for-the-socialists
[77] https://virgilwalker.substack.com/p/why-christians-must-care-about-the?. Here's a helpful defence of Christian activism and wise political engagement: https://frame-poythress.org/in-defense-of-christian-activism-vs-michael-horton-and-meredith-kline/. Plus see Appendix C in this book.

> *Charlie Kirk didn't live like that. His creed shaped every position he held, and he let the world know it without ever once apologizing or caveating it as "his truth." No, he knew that Christian truth is THE truth. Charlie's "bloody microphone" demands that we all pick it up and carry on his mission.*[78]

Without the influence of the Bible and Christianity, there would've been no William Wallace and no free Scotland. As the movie Braveheart portrays in that final battle:

> *I am William Wallace, and I see a whole army of my countrymen here in defiance of tyranny! You have come to fight as free men, and free men you are. What would you do with that freedom? Will you fight?*
>
> A voice cries out: '*Fight? Against that? No, we will run, and we will live.*' Wallace replies: *Aye, fight and you may die. Run and you'll live, at least a while. And dying in your beds many years from now, would you be willing to trade all the days from this day to that for one chance, just one chance to come back here and tell our enemies that they may take our lives, but they'll never take our freedom!*

Praise God for raising up Charlie Kirk to be a 21st-century Braveheart for Christ and for his country. May his tribe increase both at home and abroad.

---

[78] https://www.standingforfreedom.com/2025/09/18/yes-charlie-kirk-is-a-christian-martyr/

(5) Freedom Requires Co-Belligerency

Can We Unite With Catholics, Mormons, Hindus & Gays?

In the wake of Charlie Kirk's murder and a conservative resurgence in the USA, there are new calls for reconciling Protestants, Catholics, Mormons, and others (especially when both the 2nd and 3rd in command are Catholics – Vance & Rubio).[79] Meanwhile, others are calling for believers to come out and be separate from any political alliances with unbelievers.[80]

How do we resist the temptation of ecumenism yet love our neighbour? How can we biblically distinguish between church unity and civil cooperation, not mistaking engagement in an earthly sphere for endorsement in religious belief?[81] We'll look at legitimate and illegitimate cooperation with unbelievers, all hinging upon the *purpose* for which we are uniting.

Often!

We all unite with unbelievers – in sports (both playing and coaching), hobbies and recreation, business, military service, medical teams, some schooling, neighbourhood watch (due to high crime levels, Community Police Forums are very useful in South Africa), residents' associations, maintaining public spaces (parks, road repair, litter removal, etc.),

---

[79] https://x.com/5Solas2/status/1972590548088229908;
https://twitter.com/BasedMikeLee/status/1972528035862597821.
[80] https://blogs.crossmap.com/stories/revival-or-reaction-discernment-in-the-wake-of-charlie-kirks-assassination-1KOWD1-PNHD2XQVdBS0bu?utm_source=chatgpt.com.
[81] With thanks to Joey DeRuntz for his excellent work on this:
https://www.mastersbiblechurch.com/blog/a-rejoinder-to-don-green-a-biblical-and-theological-defense-of-co-belligerency.

disaster relief, firefighting, testifying in court or serving on a jury, and much more.[82]

Voting is a partnership with others in a democracy for the benefit of your fellow-imager bearers and countrymen (Gen. 1:26-28; 9:6; Jam. 3:9). As Charlie Kirk's pastor, Rob McCoy, likes to say, "Unless Jesus Christ is running for office, you're always voting for the lesser of two evils."[83]

Pagan rulers are "ministers of God" to restrain evil, uphold law and order, preserve peace and justice, and do good for a land, as part of His common grace (e.g., Pharoah, Nebuchadnezzar, Cyrus, etc.; Rom. 13:4). Joseph partnered with Pharoah to save lives during a famine (Gen. 41). Daniel served faithfully under pagan kings in Babylon (Dan. 1-6). David united with the Philistines to pursue a common enemy (1 Sam. 29; 1 Chron. 12). Yet in each case, these godly men did not compromise their faith. Christians can stand with secular rulers in the civic realm while refusing to bow to their idols. Charlie Kirk was a heroic example of this in both godly patriotism and bold witness.

God's Word urges us not to isolate but to have non-Christian friends (1 Cor. 5:10; 10:27). The salt must have actual contact with our decaying society, and the lampstand must be inside the dark room to illumine (Matt. 5:13-16). Neither our salt or our light should be shut up in a "cellar of separatism".[84] Christians should be the best citizens and most loving neighbours, treating others the way we would want to be treated

---

[82] Some of these are roles & vocations recognised explicitly in Scripture: Luke 3:14 (soldiers); Col 3:22 (employers & employees); 4:14 (medical), etc.
[83] https://www.youtube.com/watch?v=l1PdXmbgxCA;
https://www.frc.org/blog/2022/04/should-evangelicals-be-single-issue-voters-proposal-pinnacle-issue-voting#gsc.tab=0;
https://christoverall.com/article/concise/one-issue-voting-revisited/;
https://wng.org/opinions/stewarding-your-vote-1728381273;
https://www.thegospelcoalition.org/blogs/kevin-deyoung/what-am-i-doing-when-i-vote/
[84] Ibid, De Runtz.

(Matt. 7:12). Praise God for faithful Pastor John Newton and the Olney Baptist Church that produced a righteous parliamentarian like William Wilberforce to overturn the entire transatlantic slave trade!

Joey De Runtz explains:

> *Francis Schaeffer, seeing the rise of secular totalitarianism and moral collapse* [in the 1970s], *coined the term "cobelligerent" to describe those who fight the same enemy on a specific front, but do not share the same theology. An "ally" shares your faith; a "co-belligerent" shares your enemy. In* A Christian Manifesto, *Schaeffer warned that silence in the face of evil is itself evil. This is biblical (Prov. 31:8-9; Isa. 1:17; Ezek. 33; Eph. 5:11).*
>
> *If Christians refuse to act unless the cause is carried entirely by regenerate saints, they surrender the civil sphere to Satan. If the state legalizes murder, and Muslims, Catholics, and secularists all protest while evangelicals remain silent—who is more faithful to the image of God? If we refuse co-belligerency, we fail to love our neighbor.*[85]

For Example

If my Catholic or Mormon friend wants to defend human dignity, monogamy, two genders, the death penalty, limited government, or a free market, I stand with them. When my unsaved neighbour (whether gay or straight) protests socialism, tyranny, corruption, abortion, or sex-trafficking, I will say 'amen'. I will thank God for every instrument of His common grace and reflection of His Law written on human hearts (Isa. 44:28; 45:1; Rom. 2:14-15), all the while seeking to evangelise these same neighbours as we work together in the civic realm.

---

[85] https://www.mastersbiblechurch.com/blog/a-rejoinder-to-don-green-a-biblical-and-theological-defense-of-co-belligerency.

Our church in South Africa linked arms temporarily with charismatics and Muslims in a lawsuit against the state for violating constitutional religious liberties and shutting down church services during Covid, for which our whole nation suffered in a myriad of ways. This court case also afforded us evangelistic opportunities along the way with our co-belligerents.

Likewise, Christian apologist, Voddie Baucham, had a long-standing friendship with Mormon, Glenn Beck, and would speak on Beck's talk show or at political rallies together as fellow freedom fighters. Yet privately Voddie would surely evangelise Beck, and Voddie's rejection of the false Christ of Mormonism was no secret.[86]

I remember as a boy helping make and display campaign signs for my father as he ran for a local city council position for the good of my beloved hometown of Katy, Texas. My family knew that if Dad (a respected, local Christian veterinarian) won that election, he would link arms with other leaders in a civic realm, yet never presuming that they shared the same faith.

Whether then our co-belligerency is done occasionally as churches, or more often as individual Christians as we have opportunity, we can do so with a clear conscience for love of God and country.

Disclaimers

I would not see such partnerships as syncretism, ecumenism, or being unequally yoked, but rather as being a good neighbour and a responsible citizen, seeking to "do good to all people" (Gal. 6:10; 1 Thess. 5:15). To demand perfect agreement in religion before working together politically is asking for heaven on earth, which will only come when Christ returns with His perfect monarchy.

---

[86] https://www.christianpost.com/news/voddie-baucham-says-he-wont-watch-the-chosen.html?utm_source=chatgpt.com

No doubt, co-belligerency will be messy and taxing at times and will require much prayerful discernment and seeking wise counsel (Php. 1:9-11; Eph. 5:10; Prov. 11:4; 15:22). We must be willing to walk away if we cannot continue such cooperation in good conscience, fearing God over man (Prov. 29:25; Gal. 1:10).

Yet our chief aim as believers is not any earthly realm but the invisible, heavenly realm – to "seek first His kingdom" (Matt. 6:33). We pour our greatest energies and efforts into what is eternal, not temporal (2 Cor. 4:18; Col. 3:2). As John Piper says, "Christians want to alleviate all suffering, especially eternal suffering."[87]

To that end, our closest partnerships are with fellow believers in the cause of the Great Commission (Matt. 28:18-20). Nothing is more useful to our society than to see hearts changed by Christ! Only when lives are transformed will communities and nations be changed in any lasting way.

Never!

We cannot have *any* spiritual or religious unity with unbelievers, nor join them in prayer breakfasts, worship services, pulpit sharing, ecumenical councils or interfaith forums, since we do not serve the same Lord. Any organisational cooperation in ministry must begin with spiritual oneness in the gospel (Jn. 17:21; Eph. 4:3-6). Doctrinal purity must precede fellowship, and we cannot soft-pedal our evangelical essentials (Jam. 3:17; 2 Cor. 4;2). A church must have nothing to do with platforming any false religion.

We are not even permitted to "greet" or "receive" false teachers who deny this gospel; they are "to be accursed" and warned against in the church (2 Jn. 9-11; Gal. 1:6-9). "What fellowship does light have with

---

[87] https://www.desiringgod.org/messages/christians-care-about-all-suffering-and-injustice.

darkness?", asked the Apostle Paul (2 Cor. 6:14-18). We cannot be "unequally yoked" in marriage, close friendships, or business ownership.[88]

Back in 1994, MacArthur and Sproul refused to sign the *Evangelicals and Catholics Together*[89] statement because it required them to accept Catholics as fellow believers, undermining the biblical gospel. Once more in 2009 Sproul and MacArthur refused to be co-belligerents with the Manhattan Declaration, despite agreeing with its moral convictions, because the definition of a Christian was (again) vague, and justification by faith alone was compromised.[90]

Don't Blur the Lines

Jesus warned that all who name His name are not necessarily true believers (Matt. 7:21-23). Christ mandates the local church to exercise His keys of the kingdom to affirm who is truly in His kingdom or not (Matt. 16:18-19; 18:15-20; 1 Tim. 3:15; 6:20-21; 2 Tim. 1:12-14). Creeds and confessions have been written for that purpose – to clearly define what it means to be a Christian. Confusion over that definition has been a fatal flaw in 20th century Christianity, as shown by Iain Murray in his modern classic, *Evangelicalism Divided*.[91]

Christ's Bride must remain pure, undefiled by false converts. This is why we 'guard the front door' of the church with careful oversight of baptism and membership. Wolves must not be allowed into our pulpits and must be removed from our pews. Sitting at a community table for civic service must never be confused with sitting at the Lord's Table as

---

[88] Which I've addressed here: https://betweentwocultures.com/2024/11/12/unequally-yoked-in-business/.
[89] https://www.gty.org/articles/A149/evangelicals-and-catholics-together.
[90] https://learn.ligonier.org/articles/the-manhattan-declaration?utm_source=chatgpt.com;%20https://www.gty.org/blogs/B091125/the-manhattan-declaration.
[91] https://www.evangelical-times.org/evangelicalism-divided/?utm_source=chatgpt.com;%20https://www.gracechurch.org/sermons/383.

the redeemed. Honouring an upright political leader or brave neighbour mustn't be conflated with receiving a new church member through baptism. Never confuse restraining evil with proclaiming Christ.

Conservative unity is emphatically not the same as Christian unity![92] The cure to Christless conservatism is not pietism or leftism (nor more moralism) but evangelising our fellow conservatives and urging them to come to Christ, the Author of liberty.

When we make it clear that our unity in the civic realm does not make us brothers in Christ, we preserve our ability to evangelise Catholics, Mormons, gays and all others who are lost and hell-bound, as we once were until the gospel came to us. Ben Shapiro says he is thankful for a free society where Christians try to convert him, a Jew.[93] J.D. Vance and Charlie Kirk had a close friendship, working together very effectively in the political realm; yet Vance testified that Kirk often tried to convince him to become a Protestant. Keeping those differences clear is the key.

Two Spheres

As Augustine wrote long ago, the city of God and the city of man are built on different foundations, serving distinct purposes.[94] We must distinguish between the common kingdoms of this world and the eternal kingdom of Christ – between what "belongs to Caesar" and what "belongs to God" (Matt. 22:21). In the civic realm, we can rejoice when Judeo-Christian principles are being recovered by a Kirk, Vance, Rubio

---

[92] https://washingtonstand.com/article/a-tale-of-two-conservatisms-at-charlie-kirks-funeral.
[93] https://churchleaders.com/news/514969-john-macarthur-ben-shapiro-tribute.html?utm_source=chatgpt.com.
[94] "Those two cities still impel people to engage in politics for radically different reasons. Those two cities inspire two different visions for American conservatism, which were evident...at Charlie Kirk's funeral."
https://washingtonstand.com/article/a-tale-of-two-conservatisms-at-charlie-kirks-funeral

or whomever. Yet in the spiritual realm, we must resist all unbiblical, ecumenical unity with Catholics, Mormons, Hindus, gays or any other false religion.

The biblical church-state distinction has been a Baptist contribution to church history and modern civilisation:

> *God established both the church and the civil government, and He gave each its own distinct sphere of operation. The government's purposes are outlined in Romans 13:1-7 and the church's purposes in Matthew 28:19-20. Neither should control the other, nor should there be an alliance between the two. Christians in a free society can properly influence government toward righteousness, which is not the same as a denomination or group of churches controlling the government. (Matthew 22:15-22; Acts 15:17-29).*[95]

Bret Laird gives this wise and well-rounded scriptural counsel:

> *We can partner politically with unbelievers, cultists, and false teachers as "co-belligerents" in the governmental sphere as long as we do not become unequally yoked with unbelievers in the church sphere. Yet...co-belligerency and guarding against ecumenism are not incompatible.*
>
> *...Proper biblical application depends on accurate analysis. If a local church had evangelicals, Mormons, Catholics, Hindus, and theological liberals speak from the pulpit during a church service, it would be a clear-cut case of ecumenism. If a political rally included the same participants, it would be a clear-cut case of co-belligerency.*[96]

---

[95] https://www.highpointbaptist.com/baptist-distinctives.
[96] https://www.facebook.com/bret.laird (on 4 Oct. 2025).

Thanks be to God for our evangelical forefathers in the faith that have fought and died for the freedoms we enjoy today in the West by upholding gospel purity while fulfilling civic duty. May we too learn the difference between the altar and the arena, so that we might serve Christ faithfully in both. May our Lord grant us much grace and wisdom to cooperate with unbelievers as needed, while uniting with believers in our highest calling of gospel advance.[97]

---

[97] I have written in greater detail here about the need to recover the doctrine of separation and about differing levels of Christian partnerships here: https://www.antiochbiblechurch.org.za/partnerships-by-tim-cantrell/.

APPENDIX A:
Charlie Kirk's Global Impact

From London to Madrid to Berlin to Rome, prayer vigils for Charlie Kirk were attended by tens of thousands of mourners, to the surprise and dismay of a post-Christian, secularised Europe (and Australia too).[98] Charlie had just completed his first Asia tour, holding high the torch for freedom in Japan and South Korea.

Add to this estimates of over 30 million *international* viewers watching the unforgettable Charlie Kirk memorial service (on 21 September 2025) – yet further evidence of a worldwide phenomenon.

* From South Korea after Charlie's death:

> *Footage from Seoul shows crowds of people, many young and visibly energized, waving American and South Korean flags, holding signs with Kirk's image, and chanting his name in defiance of the forces that seek to shut down truth through violence and censorship. The message is clear: the values Kirk stood for — free speech, individual liberty, faith, and national pride — are not just American ideals; they are human ideals.*
>
> *South Koreans, no strangers to the threat of authoritarianism from their northern neighbor, recognize the importance of preserving liberty. Many see in Kirk a modern-day Paul Revere, warning the world of the totalitarian impulse now spreading through progressive movements that demand submission to identity politics, state control, and moral relativism.*[99]

---

[98] https://dailycaller.com/2025/09/15/vigil-charlie-kirk-international-influence-assassination-uk/

[99] https://townhall.com/tipsheet/saraharnold/2025/09/13/we-are-charlie-kirk-south-koreans-take-to-the-streets-in-global-show-of-support-n2663301. Note how pietism and ignorance are currently hindering the South Korean Church from confronting a

* From Benjamin Netanyahu:

Charlie Kirk was murdered for speaking truth and defending freedom. A lion-hearted friend of Israel, he fought the lies and stood tall for Judeo-Christian civilization. ...We lost an incredible human being. His boundless pride in America and his valiant belief in free speech will leave a lasting impact.

* From Chief Rabbi Goldstein of South Africa:

The assassination of Charlie Kirk is as disturbing and historically significant as that of the great American Presidents and leaders, who symbolized their era. The power of the movement and ideas he championed represent the great ideological battle of our times.

The gunman and his allies, like those who killed Lincoln and JFK, RFK and Martin Luther King, tried to use violence to silence their ideas. A free society cannot allow violence to succeed in the battle for ideas, which must only be waged with words. Kirk inspired a generation of young people around the world with Biblical values of faith, family and responsibility.

We must all come forward to carry the torch that the assassin sought to extinguish. And as we say in Jewish tradition: May God comfort the mourners - Charlie's bereft widow and children - among the other mourners of Zion and Jerusalem.

* From Philip Rosenthal of Christian View Network, Cape Town, South Africa:

---

new wave of communist-sympathetic rulers:
https://www.christianitytoday.com/2025/04/south-korea-impeachment-president-evangelical-reconciliation/; https://www.christianitytoday.com/2025/06/south-korea-election-evangelicals-church-politics-communism/?utm_source=chatgpt.com;
https://caliber.az/en/post/christianity-s-influence-in-south-korea.

Murdered activist Charlie Kirk was pro-life, pro-Israel, pro-marriage, pro-religious freedom, pro-free market, and a member of an evangelical church. Islamo-woke opponents of Western Civilization, both activists and media, repeatedly mis-framed him before and after his murder as a 'right wing', 'extremist', 'fascist' because he challenged their narrative, as they do the rest of evangelical Christianity and defenders of Western civilisation, likely contributing to his murder. He was accused of "Xenophobia" for his criticism of political Islam, failing to distinguish between ideology and ethnicity.

Many media articles frame him as a 'Christian nationalist' although he did not self-describe this way, but rather opposed the woke misinterpretation of the American constitution, on the question of the separation of church and state. The term 'conservative' is perhaps more appropriate, although they use it disparagingly. The views of Charlie Kirk were held by just about everyone in the history of America until the advent of the Islamo-woke left, who are still a minority but are dominating the campuses and media space. We need to oppose woke anti-Christian hate rhetoric.

* From Jaco De Beer, pastor in Cape Town, South Africa:

Yesterday, Daily Maverick published an article by Rebecca Davis claiming that the whole Charlie Kirk incident has no bearing on South Africa. I believe she is completely wrong.

What is happening in America with DEI (Diversity, Equity, Inclusion) is exactly what is happening in South Africa with B-BBEE and radical B-BBEE. The same thought patterns and justifications lie behind both systems.
If you watch Charlie Kirk's argumentation on DEI in America, you will see the parallels. His reasoning exposes the flaws of DEI in a way that applies directly to our situation here in South

Africa. The counter-arguments he makes are exactly the same as those we need to consider when it comes to B-BBEE.

...Kirk was not just another victim of violence. He was assassinated because he stood publicly for Christ, for the gospel, for the created order of God — family, marriage, truth, and the Lordship of Jesus. He was hated because he stood directly against the false woke spirit of the age.

That is why this moment matters. It is a picture of the culture war raging across the world. Behind his death is the same hatred that drives rebellion against God's truth: the rejection of His order in creation, the mockery of His design for man and woman, the suppression of His Word, the rage of a world set against Christ. This is not only America's problem. This same spirit of wokeism, radical gender ideology, and cultural Marxism is felt in South Africa too.

Genesis 3:15 reminds us that from the beginning, there has been enmity between the seed of the serpent and the seed of the woman. The Charlie Kirk assassination is another chapter in that long war — Antichrist against Christ, darkness against light. And while we mourn many deaths daily here at home, we must not miss the spiritual signpost in this one: the world hates Christ, but Christ has overcome the world.

* From Lennox Kalifungwa, a Zambian Christian leader who attended the Charlie Kirk Memorial Service in Arizona:

I feel profoundly privileged to have witnessed everything that I saw. To see the name of Christ being lifted up. To see the gospel being front and centre of so much. To see politicians not pushing their Christianity to the fringes but bringing it to the forefront – that was powerful.

To see forgiveness on full display. That moment when Erika Kirk spoke about forgiving the assassin that murdered her husband – was powerful and unbelievable! ...People seem to be reckoning with truth, and reckoning with the meaning of life, and what it means to live life in a way that really matters.

Charlie lived a life of true meaning because it was rooted in Christ, rooted in what is true. And he lived his life without apology. He didn't seek permission from anyone but his King to do what he did.

This should invigorate all of us to live our lives to the full, and not just treat our faith like a private affair. Christianity does not belong in the fringes, because Christ the Lord is King. That means everything that we do, everything we pursue, should be aimed at the highest glory of God.

It is time for us to seize this moment truly to disciple nations. To seize this moment to really bring about reformation in a profound way. Just a little light has the power to devastate the greatest darkness. If Charlie's one light was so potent that his enemies couldn't stand it, how much more powerful collectively if we all as Christians assumed our duty to speak the truth unashamedly.[100]

* From Vishal Mangalwadi, well-known Indian Christian author and leader:[101]

Charlie Kirk confronted universities because he knew that although K-12 education is essential, it is insufficient to reform the USA. Charlie's assassin seems to have grown up in a good home. It was the university that turned him into a murderer. Prof.

---

[100] https://www.facebook.com/share/r/176deThspH/
[101] https://www.facebook.com/VishaMangalwadi

Scott Masson of Tyndale University in Toronto summarizes the problem:

"The problem that Charlie Kirk was confronting was the institutionalized wickedness of a demonically false view of language and human nature that has embedded itself in the university for at least a generation. ...I saw Charlie Kirk as an ambassador to the radicalized university campuses. And the ambassador has been assassinated.

"But the enemy is not flesh and blood (though the shooter needs to be caught and brought to justice), it's the literary theories that preclude the possibility of the sort of dialogue Charlie Kirk was trying to foster, to no small degree of success.

"Charlie was a martyr to the truth, and he pointed directly to Jesus Christ, who is the way, the truth, and the life. I'm thankful for Charlie's courageous life and witness. May his death be the 'turning point' for many to follow in his Master's footsteps."

Prof. Masson is right. In order to understand his analysis, you may need to read Gene Edward Veith's study "Modern Fascism" (Concordia Press). . . Adolf Hitler did not build the Gas Chambers that burnt millions of innocent people. They were built and managed by university graduates — scientists, engineers, architects, chemists, doctors, administrators, police officers, military and judges!

Decades before coming to power, Hitler was confident of Fascism's victory because (he said) of the success of their theories in the universities. Veith provides ample evidence that American universities have been teaching Fascism, defined as "Active resistance to transcendence." There is no fear of God in post-truth universities because no God has commanded, "You *shall not kill." That means, there is no inalienable "Right to life," of a pre-born child or a champion of civility.*

Charlie Kirk was right: America needs a reformation which will replace university's fascist worldview with God's truth. ...A few years ago, Charlie was given a copy of my book, <u>The Book that Made Your World: How the Bible Created the Soul of Western Civilisation</u>. After devouring it, Charlie would often say to others, "The Bible created the soul of America!"

Media Statement
11 September 2025

LEX LIBERTAS MOURNS THE PASSING OF CHARLIE KIRK

Pretoria — It is truly inspiring to witness the profound impact Charlie Kirk has had during his short life. To say that he was "one in a million" would be an understatement—it would fail to capture the extraordinary calibre of the man he was.

Charlie was known for his unwavering faith in God and in Jesus Christ, his deep love for his family, and his steadfast commitment to his nation. He dedicated himself not only to the preservation of Western civilization but to the very idea of civilization itself.

Through his sacrifice, Charlie became a modern-day Hector of Troy—a man who charged into the fray, fully aware of the danger, yet compelled by a deep love for his family and all the things he sought to defend. We mourn his passing.

But the appropriate response is not to retreat—it is to advance. It is to pick up the torch that Charlie has laid down. It is to embody the courage he so often called for. Courage in defense of all that is true, good, and beautiful—so that we may pass it on to those who come after us.

"I do not love the bright sword for its sharpness, nor the arrow for its swiftness, nor the warrior for his glory. I love only that which they defend."
— J.R.R. Tolkien

Lex Libertas is a think tank and advocacy group working towards a viable political dispensation in South Africa, based on the principles of freedom, decentralisation, and self-governance.

APPENDIX B:
A Prayer for America from Africa[102]

My wife and I are Americans who have now lived more of our lives on African soil than on American soil. All five of our kids were born in Africa, and we are willing to be buried in Africa for the sake of Christ and His kingdom. We love our adopted home nation of South Africa, and see her great potential for impact on the African continent and beyond!

Yet we still also love and pray often for our native land, the United States of America, and we realise the tremendous impact she has on the world for better or for worse. The longer we live overseas, the more deeply we appreciate what America once stood for, unlike any other nation in history. We yearn for more of those same liberties, and more of human dignity to be enjoyed by our South African neighbours.

In 1862, in the middle of the Civil War, President Abraham Lincoln called the United States "the last, best hope on earth". As Christians, we do not look to earth at all for our hopes – our hope and our "citizenship is in heaven, from which also we eagerly wait for a Saviour, the Lord Jesus Christ" (Php. 3:20). King Jesus does not need America or any other nation; He "will build His Church" and His Great Commission will prevail in the end (Matt. 16:18; 24:14)!

Yet as far as earthly prospects for freedom and security in the world, we dare not underestimate the vital role of the USA, and the massive benefits and generosity that it has brought to global missions and much more.

---

[102] By Tim Cantrell on July 4th 2025, originally published here: https://thecripplegate.com/a-prayer-from-africa-for-america/. This seems to capture Charlie's heartbeat and passion in many ways – a kindred spirit to me, though we never met. I look forward to thanking him in Heaven.

Anders Rasmussen, a Danish politician, states:

> *Only America has the diplomatic reach, the financial resources, and the firepower to lead the free world against the autocrats, rogue states, and terrorists that are trying to overwhelm it. As the Prime Minister of Denmark from 2001 to 2009, and the Secretary-General of NATO from 2009 to 2014, I know how important American leadership is. I've seen firsthand what happens when America tries to lead from behind instead of leading from the front.*
>
> *...Europe is too weak and divided to lead the world. The free nations have an essential role to play, and they must shoulder their full share of the cost, but only America has the credibility to lead. This is not just about money or manpower. It is also about morality. Only America has the moral greatness to lead the free world—not for the sake of power, but for the sake of peace.*
>
> *...An American retreat will unleash a new plague of dictators and oppressors who seek to undo all the good America has done to secure peace and prosperity around the world for decades.*

Pastor Tommy Nelson sums up well the history and legacy of the USA, from a Christian perspective:

> *...our American forefathers...left us with a Christian, biblical perspective of God, as outside of government, to Whom government is subservient. Of God in a biblical sense, not just a G-O-D idea, but the God of the Jew, the infinite personal God who has made himself known and redeemed man through Jesus Christ. ...They understood that human rights were taken from nature's God, of "life and liberty and the pursuit of happiness".*
>
> *And so, we had a government that was legislative, judicial, and*

executive, each branch checking the others. Nobody was sovereign, all checked by the Constitution. ...It was an idea that sprang out of the Protestant Reformation, concerning God and man and how he should live and be governed.

Our country had problems, and our problems did not come from the inherent flaws of our system. Our problems came because of a national lack of courage to live out our Constitution. The idea of racism and the Jim Crow laws were unconstitutional. They existed not because of our belief system, but because of our lack of national courage to get rid of them!

...Everybody wanted (and still wants) to come to America; we greet them in the harbour with a Lady Liberty holding her torch...that Lady of Light and glory that awaits you in the harbor, with these words inscribed upon her (by Jewish poet, Emma Lazarus): "Give me your tired, your poor, your huddled masses yearning to be free. The wretched refuse of your teeming shore, send these, the homeless, tempest-tossed to me. I lift my lamp beside the golden door."

Dennis Prager describes America's founding Judeo-Christian values:

...[These values] can and must be adopted by every nation and culture in the world; Americans must relearn and recommit to these values, and...vigorously export them. For if the world does not adopt [these core] values, the result will be chaos and barbarism on an unprecedented scale.

...America is the only country that was founded not on a race, ethnicity, or nationality, but on an idea: limited government— because the founders of America believed, first and foremost, in liberty. America became the freest country in world history, which is why France gave the Statue of Liberty to one country: America. And America has given more liberty and opportunity to more people from more nations than any country in world history.

Yes, America allowed slavery in half of its states. But every society in the world practiced slavery. What rendered America unique is that Americans killed one another in its bloodiest war to abolish slavery, and that it eventually became the least racist, most multi-racial country in history.

How then should Christians in Africa, or anywhere, pray for the USA? Pray that she would repent and turn to Christ! Pray that she would return to the God of her fathers and to the one Book that made her great, the Word of God. Pray that she would repent of all her shameful slaughter of infants, wanton immorality, sexual perversity, and arrogant pride.

Pray that she could once more be a beacon of hope, light, and liberty to the nations of the world for the glory of God. Pray that God would awaken His Church in the USA to be the "pillar and support of the truth" that she is called to be (1 Tim. 3:15), to preach and practice the Bible faithfully and fearlessly.

A few years ago, I heard a Russian Christian say to an American pastor: "We are a country in the darkness and we are looking for light. You are a country in the light and you are searching for the dark." May God have mercy on the United States of America.

O beautiful for spacious skies,
For amber waves of grain,
For purple mountain majesties
Above the fruited plain!
America! America!
God shed His grace on thee,
And crown thy good with brotherhood
From sea to shining sea.

O beautiful for pilgrim feet,
Whose stern, impassioned stress
A thoroughfare for freedom beat
Across the wilderness!
America! America!
God mend thine every flaw,
Confirm thy soul in self-control,
Thy liberty in law.
(Katherine Lee Bates, 1893)

APPENDIX C:
Grudem's Case for a Public Theology

Should Christians try to influence laws and politics?[103]

The "significant influence" view says that Christians *should* seek to influence civil government according to God's moral standards and God's purposes for government as revealed in the Bible (when rightly understood). But while Christians exercise this influence, they must simultaneously insist on protecting freedom of religion for all citizens.

1. Old Testament support for significant Christian influence

The Bible shows several examples of believers in God who influenced secular governments.

For instance, the Jewish prophet Daniel exercised a strong influence on the secular government in Babylon. Daniel said to Nebuchadnezzar,

> "Therefore, O king, let my counsel be acceptable to you: *break off your sins* by *practicing righteousness*, and your iniquities by *showing mercy to the oppressed*, that there may perhaps be a lengthening of your prosperity" (Dan. 4:27).

Daniel's approach is bold and clear. It is the opposite of a modern multicultural approach that might say something like this:

---

[103] After Grudem gives a detailed refutation of five other popular-but-flawed Christian views, this is now his conclusion, taken from: https://www.waynegrudem.com/wp-content/uploads/2014/05/Why-Christians-should-influence-government-booklet.pdf. On this subject, see also two other excellent introductions and overviews: https://christoverall.com/article/concise/the-gospels-irreducibly-political-message/; https://christoverall.com/article/longform/what-is-the-spectrum-of-major-views-on-political-theology-a-proposed-taxonomy-of-seven-views-on-religion-and-government/.

"O King Nebuchadnezzar, I am a Jewish prophet, but I would not presume to impose my Jewish moral standards on your Babylonian kingdom. Ask your astronomers and your soothsayers! They will guide you in your own traditions. Then follow your own heart! It would not be my place to speak to you about right and wrong."

No, Daniel boldly told the king, *"Break off your sins* by practicing righteousness, and your iniquities by showing mercy to the oppressed."

At that time, Daniel was a high official in Nebuchadnezzar's court. He was "ruler over the whole province of Babylon" and "chief prefect over all the wise men of Babylon" (Dan. 2:48). He was regularly "at the king's court" (v. 49). Therefore, it seems that Daniel had a significant advisory role to the king.

This leads to a reasonable assumption that, though it is not specified in the text, Daniel's summary statement about "sins" and "iniquities" and "showing mercy to the oppressed" (Dan. 4:27), was followed by a longer conversation in which Daniel named specific policies and actions of the king that were either good or evil in the eyes of God.

The counsel that Jeremiah proclaimed to the Jewish exiles in Babylon also supports the idea of believers having influence on laws and government. Jeremiah told these exiles, *"Seek the welfare of the city* where I have sent you into exile, and pray to the LORD on its behalf, for in its welfare you will find your welfare" (Jer. 29:7).

But if believers are to seek to bring good to such a pagan society, that must include seeking to bring good to its government (as Daniel did). The true "welfare" of such a city will be advanced through governmental laws and policies that are consistent with God's teaching in the Bible, not by those that are contrary to the Bible's teachings.

Other believers in God also had high positions of governmental influence in non-Jewish nations. Joseph was the highest official after Pharaoh, king of Egypt, and had great influence in the decisions of Pharaoh (see Gen. 41:37–45; 42:6; 45:8–9, 26). Later, Moses boldly stood before the Pharaoh and demanded freedom for the people of Israel, saying, "Thus says the LORD, 'Let my people go'" (Exod. 8:1).

Nehemiah was "cupbearer to the king" (Neh. 1:11), a position of high responsibility before King Artaxerxes of Persia.[104] Mordecai "was second in rank to King Ahasuerus" of Persia (Esth. 10:3; see also 9:4). Queen Esther also had significant influence on the decisions of Ahasuerus (see Esth. 5:1–8; 7:1–6; 8:3–13; 9:12–15, 29–32).

In addition, there are several passages in the Old Testament prophets that address the sins of foreign nations around Israel: see Isaiah 13–23; Ezekiel 25–32; Amos 1–2; Obadiah (addressed to Edom); Jonah (sent to Nineveh); Nahum (addressed to Nineveh); Habakkuk 2; Zephaniah 2. These prophets could speak to nations outside of Israel because the God who is revealed in the Bible is the God of *all peoples* and *all nations* of the earth.

Therefore, the moral standards of God as revealed in the Bible are the moral standards to which God will hold all people accountable. This includes more than the way people conduct themselves in their marriages and families, in their neighborhoods and schools, and in their jobs and businesses. It also concerns the way people conduct themselves *in government offices*.

Believers have a responsibility to bear witness to the moral standards of the Bible by which God will hold all people accountable, including those in public office.

---

[104] "The position of cupbearer to the king was a high office and involved regular access to the king," ESV Study Bible (Wheaton, IL: Crossway, 2008), 825.

2. New Testament support for significant Christian influence

A New Testament example of influence on government is found in the life of John the Baptist. During his lifetime, the ruler of Galilee (from 4 BC to AD 39) was Herod Antipas, a "tetrarch" who had been appointed by the Roman emperor and was subject to the authority of the Roman Empire. Matthew's Gospel tells us that John the Baptist rebuked Herod for a specific personal sin in his life:

> For Herod had seized John and bound him and put him in prison for the sake of Herodias, his brother Phillip's wife, because John had been saying to him, "It is not lawful for you to have her" (Matt. 14:3–4).

But Luke's Gospel adds more detail:

> [John the Baptist] preached good news to the people. But Herod the tetrarch, who had been reproved by him for Herodias, his brother's wife, *and for all the evil things that Herod had done*, added this to them all, that he locked up John in prison (Luke 3:18–20).

Certainly "all the evil things that Herod had done" included evil actions that he had carried out as a governing official in the Roman Empire. John the Baptist rebuked him *for all of them.* He boldly spoke to officials of the empire about the moral right and wrong of their governmental policies. In doing this, John was following in the steps of Daniel and many Old Testament prophets. The New Testament portrays John the Baptist's actions as those of "a righteous and holy man" (Mark 6:20). He is an excellent example of a believer who had what I call "significant influence" on the policies of a government (though it cost him his life: see Mark 6:21–29).

Another example is the apostle Paul. While Paul was in prison in Caesarea, he stood trial before the Roman governor Felix. Here is what happened:

> After some days, Felix came with his wife Drusilla, who was Jewish, and he sent for Paul and heard him speak about faith in Christ Jesus. And *as he reasoned about righteousness and self-control and the coming judgment*, Felix was alarmed and said, "Go away for the present. When I get an opportunity, I will summon you" (Acts 24:24-25).

While Luke does not give us any more details, the fact that Felix was "alarmed" and that Paul reasoned with him about "righteousness" and "the coming judgment" indicates that Paul was talking about moral standards of right and wrong and the ways in which Felix, as an official of the Roman Empire, had obligations to live up to the standards that are given by God.

Paul no doubt told Felix that he would be accountable for his actions at "the coming judgment" and that this was what led Felix to be "alarmed." When Luke tells us that Paul "reasoned" with Felix about these things, the word (Greek *dialegomai*) indicates a back-and-forth conversation or discussion.

It is not difficult to suppose that Felix asked Paul, "What about this decision that I made? What about this policy? What about this ruling?" It would be an artificial restriction on the meaning of the text to suppose that Paul *only* spoke with Felix about his "private" life and not about his actions as a Roman governor. Paul is thus another example of attempting to exercise "significant Christian influence" on civil government.

Clearly, examples of godly believers' influence on governments are not minor or confined to obscure portions of the Bible but are found in Old Testament history from Genesis all the way to Esther (the last historical book), in the canonical writing prophets from Isaiah to Zephaniah, and in the New Testament in both the Gospels and Acts. And those are just the examples of God's servants bringing significant influence" to pagan kings who gave no allegiance to the God of Israel or to Jesus in the New Testament times.

If we add to this list the many stories of Old Testament prophets bringing counsel and encouragement and rebuke to the good and evil kings of Israel as well, then we would include the histories of all the kings and the writings of all the prophets—nearly every book of the Old Testament. And we could add in several passages from Psalms and Proverbs that speak of good and evil rulers. Influencing government for good on the basis of the wisdom found in God's own words is a theme that runs through the entire Bible.

3. Romans 13 and 1 Peter 2

In addition to these examples, *specific Bible passages that teach about government* present an argument for "significant Christian influence." Why do we think God put Romans 13:1–7 and 1 Peter 2:13–14 and other related passages (as in Psalms and Proverbs) in the Bible? Are they in the Bible simply as a matter of intellectual curiosity for Christians who will read them privately but never use them to speak to government officials about how God understands their roles and responsibilities? Does God intend this material to be *concealed* from people in government and *kept secret* by Christians who read it and silently moan about "how far government has strayed from what God wants it to be"?

Certainly God put such passages there not only to inform Christians about how *they* should relate to civil government, but also in order that *people with governmental responsibilities* could know what God himself expects from them. This also pertains to other passages in the Bible that instruct us about God's moral standards, about the nature and purpose of human beings made in God's image, about God's purposes for the earth, and about principles concerning good and bad governments.

All of these teachings are relevant for those who serve in governmental office, and we should speak and teach about them when we have opportunity to do so.

4. The responsibility of citizens in a democracy to understand the Bible's teaching

There is still another argument for "significant Christian influence" on government that applies to anyone who lives in a democracy, because in a democracy a significant portion of the ruling power of government is entrusted to the citizens generally, through the ballot box. Therefore all citizens who are old enough to vote have a *responsibility* before God to know what God expects of civil government and what kind of moral and legal standards he wants government to follow. But *how can citizens learn what kind of government God is seeking?* They can learn this only if churches teach about government and politics from the Bible.

I realize that pastors will differ in the degree of detail they wish to teach with regard to specific political issues facing a nation (for example, whether to teach about issues such as abortion, euthanasia, care for the poor, the military and national defense, use and care of the environment, or the nature of marriage). But surely it is a responsibility of pastors to teach on *some* of these specific policies in ways that go beyond the mere statement, "You have a responsibility to vote intelligently."

After all, who else is going to teach these Christians about *exactly how* the Bible applies to specific political issues? Would pastors think it right to leave their congregations with such vague guidance in other areas of life? Would we say, "You have a responsibility to bring up your children according to Christian principles," and then never explain to them what those Christian principles are? Would we think it right to say to people in the business world, "You have a responsibility to work in the business world according to Christian principles," and then never give them any details about what these Christian principles are?

No, the responsibility of pastors is to give wise biblical teaching, *explaining exactly how the teachings of the Bible apply to various specific situations in life*, and that should certainly include instruction about some policy matters in government and politics.

Final Thoughts

There is a view among a few Christians in the United States today called "Theonomy." Theonomists argue that the Old Testament laws that God gave to Israel in the Mosaic covenant should be the pattern for civil laws in nations today. This would include carrying out the death penalty for such things as blasphemy or adultery or homosexual conduct!

The error of Theonomists is that they misunderstand the unique place that these laws for Israel had in the history of the whole Bible, and they misunderstand the New Testament teaching of the distinction between the realm of the church and the realm of the state that Jesus established when he said, "Render to Caesar the things that are Caesar's, and to God the things that are God's" (Matt. 22:21).

Furthermore, when I speak about "significant Christian influence" on government, I want to be very clear that *I do not mean that Christians should only vote for other Christian candidates for office*, or even that Christians should generally prefer an evangelical candidate over others who are running. The relevant principle is this: Christians should support candidates who best represent moral and political values consistent with biblical teaching, no matter their religious background or convictions.

Two concluding observations: First, without Christian influence, governments will have no clear moral compass; and second, Christian citizens have an obligation to exercise such influence.

1. Without Christian Influence, Governments Will Have No Clear Moral Compass

Try to imagine what a nation and its government would be like *if all Christian influence on government were suddenly removed.* Within a few years no one would have any moral absolutes beyond their individual moral sentiments and moral intuitions, which can be so unreliable. In addition, most people would have no moral authority beyond that of individual human opinion. Therefore, how could a nation find any moral guidance?

Consider the many political issues facing the United States (and other nations) that have significant moral components to them. For example: war, same-sex marriage, abortion, pornography, poverty, care for the environment, capital punishment, and public education. There are many other issues as well. The United States has a tremendous need for moral guidance, and I am convinced that Christians should study and discuss and then speak publicly about them.

If pastors and church members say, "I'll let somebody else speak about that," where will the nation's moral standards come from? Where will people learn about ethics? Perhaps from Hollywood movies? From friends at work or at the local bar? From professional counselors? From elementary school teachers? But where do *these* people learn about right and wrong?

The simple fact is that if Christians do not speak publicly about what the Bible teaches regarding issues of right and wrong, there aren't many other good sources for finding any transcendent source of ethics, any source outside of ourselves and our own subjective feelings and consciences.

As Christians, we need to remember that the entire world is locked in a tremendous spiritual battle. There are demonic forces, forces of Satan, that seek to oppose God's purposes and bring evil and destruction to every human being that God created in his own image, and also bring destruction to every human society and every nation.

If pastors and church members say, "I'm going to be silent about the moral and ethical issues that we face as a nation," that will leave a moral vacuum, and it will not be long until the ultimate adversaries of the Gospel—Satan and his demons—will rush in and influence every decision in a way contrary to biblical standards.

2. The political obligations of all Christian citizens

I believe that every Christian citizen who lives in a democracy has at the very least a minimal obligation to be well-informed and to vote for candidates and policies that are most consistent with biblical principles. The opportunity to help select the kind of government we will have is a *stewardship* that God entrusts to citizens in a democracy, a stewardship that we should not neglect or fail to appreciate.

Furthermore, I want to ask every Christian in the United States to consider whether he or she has a higher obligation than merely voting. The question is whether someone thinks it is morally right *to receive great benefits from a nation but to give almost nothing in return*. The great freedoms that citizens have in the United States came only as a result of great sacrifice on the part of millions of others.

The original signers of the Declaration of Independence knew that they were publicly declaring themselves to be guilty of treason against Britain, and they knew they would be subject to the death penalty and to confiscation of their property if the British caught them or defeated them.[105] Nor could they have any great confidence that they would win a war against the most powerful nation on earth at that time. Therefore the last line in the Declaration of Independence says this:

> And for the support of this declaration, with a firm reliance on the protection of divine Providence, we mutually pledge to each other our lives, our fortunes, and our sacred honor.[106]

Independence from Britain did not come cheaply. In the War of Independence, approximately 4,500 Americans died. Later wars were even more costly. All told, hundreds of thousands of men (and many women as well) *sacrificed their lives* to protect the nation and preserve the freedoms we enjoy today. Is it right that we simply enjoy these freedoms while giving back to our nation nothing in return?

Should we not participate at least at some level in giving money or giving time to support specific candidates and issues? Or writing letters or helping to distribute literature? Or even running for office or volunteering to serve in the military? Is it not right that all of us at least do something more than merely voting to preserve and protect this nation?

NOTE #1: See also a case for public theology in my book, *True Calvinism: The Hope of the World*, Chapter 7, "Every Square Inch: Living Out Christ's Lordship", showing how our faith transforms our view of culture, politics, the state, economics, law, morality and more (2025, self-published – contact me at: tim@antioch.org.za)

NOTE #2: Our Puritan forefathers defended the role of Christ in politics in the London 1689 Baptist Confession, with a whole chapter on "The Civil Magistrate" (chp. 24), which God has ordained and in

---

[105] Pauline Maier, *American Scripture: Making the Declaration of Independence* (New York: Alfred A. Knopf, 1998), 59, 118, 125, 147, 152.
[106] Declaration of Independence, adopted July 4, 1776.
www.archives.gov/national_archives_experience/charters/declaration_transcript.html.

which some Christians should serve honourably. As Sam Waldron writes, "To restrict Christianity to the 'spiritual' realm is, ultimately, to destroy it."[107]

POSTSCRIPT – Jim Elliot Parallels

I'm struck again by the comparisons between Jim Elliot and Charlie Kirk. Still in his twenties, Jim wrote these lines below (in his journals and letters), which have impacted me deeply since my youth:[108]

Father, make of me a crisis man. Bring those I contact to decision. Let me not be a milepost on a single road; make me a fork, that men must turn one way or another on facing Christ in me.

Father take my life, even my blood, if Thou wilt, and consume it with Thine enveloping fire. I would not save it, for it is not mine to save. Have it Lord, have it all. Pour my life as an oblation for the world. Blood is only of value as it flows before Thine altars.

God, I pray Thee, light these idle sticks of my life, that I may burn for Thee. Consume my life, my God, for it is Thine. <u>I seek not a long life, but a full one, like You, Lord Jesus.</u>

---

[107] p. 284, *A Modern Exposition of the 1689 Baptist Confession of Faith.*
[108] https://inkindle.wordpress.com/2010/12/05/a-heart-on-fire-kindling-from-jim-elliot/.

THE GOSPEL: The Pathway to Ultimate Freedom

Why does Christianity lift highest the freedom torch? Why has the Bible had such powerful impact in history for human dignity and civil liberties, more than all other world religions combined?

Because there is nothing more pro-freedom than the gospel of our risen Lord Jesus, as Charlie Kirk often proclaimed. *Here is the greatest news in the entire universe – a brief summary of the biblical gospel, of what it means to be a Christian, the true way of salvation:*

Being a Christian is more than identifying yourself with a particular religion or affirming a certain value system. Being a Christian means you have embraced what the Bible says about God, mankind, and salvation. Consider the following truths straight from Scripture[109]. Hear the Word of the Lord:

God Is Sovereign Creator

Contemporary thinking says man is the product of evolution. But the Bible says we were created by a personal God to love, serve, and enjoy endless fellowship with Him. The New Testament reveals it was Jesus Himself who created everything (Jn. 1:3; Col. 1:16). Therefore, He also owns and rules everything (Ps. 103:19). That means He has authority over our lives and we owe Him absolute allegiance, obedience, and worship.

God Is Holy

God is absolutely and perfectly holy (Isa. 6:3); therefore He cannot commit or approve of evil (Jam. 1:13). God requires holiness of us as well. God says, "You shall be holy, for I am holy" (1 Pet. 1:16).

---

[109] Adapted from: https://www.gracechurch.org/about/gospel.

Mankind Is Sinful

According to Scripture, everyone is guilty of sin: "There is no man who does not sin" (1 Kgs 8:46). That doesn't mean we're incapable of performing acts of human kindness. But we're utterly incapable of understanding, loving, or pleasing God on our own (Rom. 3:10-12). We break His holy Law (His Ten Commandments) every day in thought, word and deed, both in what is done and left undone.

Sin Demands a Penalty

God's holiness and justice demand that all sin be punished by eternal death (Ezek. 18:4; Rom. 6:23). That's why simply changing our patterns of behaviour can't solve our sin problem or eliminate its consequences.

Jesus Is Lord and Saviour

Rom. 10:9 says, "If you confess with your mouth Jesus as Lord, and believe in your heart that God raised Him from the dead, you shall be saved." Even though God's justice demands death for sin, His love has provided a Saviour who paid the penalty and died for sinners (1 Pet. 3:18). Christ's death satisfied the demands of God's justice, and Christ's perfect life satisfied the demands of God's holiness (2 Cor. 5:21), thereby enabling Him to forgive and save those who place their faith in Him (Rom. 3:26).

The Character of Saving Faith

True faith is always accompanied by repentance from sin. Repentance is agreeing with God that you are sinful, confessing your sins to Him, and making a conscious choice to turn from sin (Luke 13:3, 5; 1 Thess. 1:9), pursue Christ (Matt. 11: 28-30; Jn. 17:3), and obey Him (1 Jn. 2:3).

It isn't enough to believe certain facts about Christ. Even Satan and his demons believe in the true God (Jam. 2:19), but they don't love and obey Him. True saving faith always responds in obedience (Eph. 2:10).

Today is the day of salvation (2 Cor. 6:2)! You can call on the Lord now and He will set you free from sin and guilt and fear. If you become a disciple of Jesus, "you will know the truth and the truth will set you free" (John 8:32).

It may cost you your life. Jesus was hated and crucified. He calls you to take up your cross and follow Him. You may be called to martyrdom like Charlie Kirk or to smaller acts of obedience; either way it will be worth it!

www.ingramcontent.com/pod-product-compliance
Lightning Source LLC
Chambersburg PA
CBHW071312040426
42444CB00009B/1993